It's Been Grand
... Now It's Final!

It's Been Grand ... Now It's Final!

Mike Stephenson and Eddie Hemmings

Vertical Editions
www.verticaleditions.com

First published in the United Kingdom in 2016 by Vertical Editions, Unit 4a, Snaygill Industrial Estate, Skipton, North Yorkshire BD23 2QR

www.verticaleditions.com

ISBN 978-1-904091-97-4

A CIP catalogue record for this book is available from the British Library

Cover design by HBA, York

Printed and bound by Jellyfish Solutions, Swanmore, Hants

For those those who have been my greatest support throughout the years – my dear wife Carole plus our children Mark, Lisa and Sharon; our four grandchildren Owen and Isabella, Eleanor and Stephen. Together they are MY family in Rugby League.

Eddie

For my family, Maureen, Craig, Hayley, Kayley, Alyssa, my brother Derek and grandchildren Holly, Archie and Harry.

Stevo

Contents

Acknowledgements

My thanks to everyone who has helped me throughout my broadcasting career. From my early days at the BBC to John Davis, my first producer at Sky, who took a punt on me when being advised to search elsewhere. To David Hill whose love of rugby league saw to it that we carried on when BSB was no more. To Vic Wakeling CBE who picked up the baton when Hilly left and has been our greatest supporter throughout. And, to Neville 'Teenage Mutant Ninja Nevvie' Smith who I've known man and boy for all these years and who is the greatest rugby league director on earth. I couldn't have done what I've done without my 'brain' Ian Proctor whose statistics and knowledge have helped me through immeasurably – he never misses a trick. Thank you to the great game of rugby league – the coaches, players and administrators – for allowing me to be part of your world, I couldn't have done it without any of you! And to my great mate Stevo without who this journey just wouldn't have been the same.

Eddie Hemmings

I would like to mention all my family, friends and colleagues who have helped and supported me over the years, first as a rugby league player and more latterly in the media. The list of names is too long to write here but you know who you are and I thank you from the bottom of my heart. Also I would like to thank everyone in rugby league, from the players and coaches to the officials and administrators. And of course, not forgetting the fans – even those who took umbrage over my comments at times – you all contribute to making the game the greatest of all. And finally a big thank you to my best friend Eddie, without your timely intervention I might be still digging holes for a living!

Mike 'Stevo' Stephenson

Foreword

Eddie and Stevo! The very names reflect a feeling of fond familiarity, respect and real affection for two outstanding characters. Two men who have brought two vital qualities to their work and to the sport of Rugby League – a depth of knowledge, along with genuine passion.

They know their sport – the clubs, the players, the big personalities – and they share the passion and involvement of the most committed rugby league fans. They did so when they first came together and they still do.

They were two of the very best signings made by Sky Sports just before we launched our first dedicated channel 25 years ago.

Eddie Hemmings was an easy choice. He had enjoyed an outstanding career with the BBC for many years and brought vast experience and much-needed credibility to a fledging service – first under the control of BSB (remember the squarial?) and then Sky and the launch of Sky Sports.

Eddie took a huge gamble when he first signed and we have been grateful ever since. In those early pioneering days, his versatility and journalistic instincts were an enormous help. His work included stints as a football commentator or touchline reporter and he almost changed the direction of Brian Clough's career from football management to cricket commentary.

Eddie heard a mention in the tunnel before a cup game at Villa Park, grabbed a mic and then got the Forest manager to talk about it live on air. Clough was serious about joining our cricket boys who were with England in the West Indies, but the switch was halted by a call from the Forest chairman a couple of days later. Clough stayed in football and Eddie switched to rugby league full-time. Good decisions by both, although sadly, Clough's career never matched his previous European trophy winning standards. Eddie simply went from strength to strength.

Mike Stephenson was a bigger risk when we signed him. Yes, he'd won the World Cup with Great Britain in 1972, but then he'd finished his career and made his home in Australia. And he wasn't the prettiest – a good face for radio!

But we at Sky, and the fans, loved him from Day One. Well, almost Day One. He loves to tell the story of giving me a "Liverpool kiss" in a Manchester bar two days before Sky made me his boss. He made my eyes water, but I didn't go down.

I had breakfast with him the following morning. Well, I had breakfast – he joined me, pint in hand, from the bar where he'd spent the entire night!

There are other tales from The Adventures of Stevo but it would be very wrong of me not to concentrate on his true talent and strengths. His dedication and love of his sport are immense. He is a real fount of knowledge on rugby league and has invested in a unique collection of memorabilia. Equally, his professionalism in the studio and commentary box override those stories of celebratory nights. His enthusiasm for the game shines through.

Stevo is always the first to pay tribute to the help he received from sidekick Eddie, and his immediate and real boss and mentor, Executive Producer Neville Smith – and so he should. He owes them both big-time.

Eddie has so often been the calming, steadying influence and we have been grateful many times for his tact and timing when he interrupts a Stevo rant to get commentary back on track. Both have strong views and opinions and they don't always agree, but we get a balanced debate. Well, most of the time.

They were together for the launch of both Sky Sports and Super League, along with its switch to a summer game. And it wasn't easy. Eddie and Stevo helped us rise above the early challenges and problems in those difficult early days and Sky Sports will always remember their enormous contribution to the success of our channels.

And, in Super League, they have enjoyed great years and great times. We all shared big nights in Paris and Charlton's Valley Stadium. Grand Final Night at Old Trafford is now a major event in the British sporting calendar and they both helped persuade me to back the play-offs against the traditional table-topping champions.

We were mid-contract when the idea was first discussed and it needed Sky approval for changes to be made. Eddie and Stevo, plus Neville Smith and other leading figures in the game, offered sage advice and the Grand Final was an instant hit.

Eddie and Stevo have been witness to, and have played a vital role, during this amazing era for their sport. They have seen great games and great players. They rose to the occasion week after week, year after year. They did it all with style, class, a sense of fun (we really are in the entertainment business) and 100 per cent commitment.

We have been lucky at Sky Sports to build the best commentary partnerships and teams in the business – Tyler and Gray on football, Harrison and Barnes on rugby union, our entire star-studded cricket line-up, Stelling and friends on *Soccer Saturday*. It adds up to an elite band of players.

Excuse the familiarity, and use of their commonly known names, but Eddie and Stevo are their equals in every respect. They have earned their places in the history of both Sky and rugby league.

Vic Wakeling CBE, Former Sky Head of Sport and Managing Director Sky Sports

1

Stevo: Meeting John Parrott

After retiring from the Penrith Panthers in 1978, I had started out in making a career In the media, a task that I knew was not going to be easy seeing as no other English player had ventured into this area in Australia – and soon after I realised not many Aussies wanted me to start either!

So I took a train to Sydney City and entered the huge offices of the *Sydney Sun* newspaper on Broadway Avenue, just a short distance from the station, and asked for a job.

Amazingly I somehow asked the receptionist if I could speak to the sports editor. And to my surprise she rang his secretary who asked me to come up to the fourth floor where I came face to face with a certain John Benaud, a former Aussie Cricket international and the brother of the Richie Benaud.

Thankfully John recognised me from the Penrith Panthers and asked me what I wanted.

"I'd like to write for your paper."

"OK, go into that spare office over there and write."

Next thing I knew they shoved a typewriter in my hands and he suggested I write a 'dummy' column.

Three hours later I walked back into his office, offered my dummy effort for him to scrutinise and he was shocked to find out I had written it out in pen on paper.

"What happened to the typing?" he enquired.

"Can't type," was my quick reply.

He looked it over and said loudly, "You want to be in journalism, can't type and yet you have written this shit?"

I stood up and started to walk out the door when he called me back and said, "Wait you don't understand, this is good shit! Are you happy to write all this about your opposition players, it's mighty strong stuff?"

"Why not I replied, I'm only being honest."

John offered me a job on the spot, dumped an old Remington typewriter into my hands and told me to take it home, learn how to use it and have 35 paragraphs of copy in this office by Wednesday morning.

And that was the start of 15 years at the *Sun* newspaper and my entry into the world of 'Make believe' or is it 'Make it up'? Either way yours truly had hustled his way into 'the fourth estate' without any background in journalism, little education and a limited ability at spelling.

I owe a lot to John and a certain Gary Lester, a senior sports writer at the paper, who gave up a lot of their spare time to help me into this strange but wonderful world of the media and I loved every minute of it. At the time I thought it was the best job in the world. Little did I know later in life there was one even better back home in Blighty.

As time went on I started doing radio work with stations 2UE, 2GB and later 2SM, just doing 'Around the Ground' bulletins yet hoping I would one day get the chance to start broadcasting games as a 'colour' commentator. Then ABC, the national broadcaster – equivalent to the BBC in the UK – gave me that chance, firstly on radio then on TV. The door had opened and I worked hard to ensure that door wouldn't be shut.

Sadly the door not only slammed shut with a shocking 'BANG', the door also fell off its hinges and my media career was finished … that was until I met a bloke with a long nose in Manchester.

Each year after the Aussie season had finished, I would fly back to the UK for about six weeks to spend time with my two children from my first marriage. The last game in the Sydney Club rounds that year was at Manly, which was close to where I lived. I was broadcasting on ABC radio and I was in buoyant mood looking forward to flying back to the UK when my co-commentator requested a favour. He asked if I would mind taking a parcel for him to London and then posting it to a certain lady he obviously had taken a shine to whilst covering the Ashes cricket for the station earlier that summer. And being such a nice bloke I agreed to take the parcel.

"It's not large so it won't cost you much in postage," he said. So I packed his missive into my luggage and flew into London.

After looking at the address, which clearly stated the BBC offices in Manchester, I decided not to post it but drive over the Pennines with it from my Mum and Dad's house in Dewsbury, barely one hour away by car.

I was intrigued as to what my co-commentator's lady friend looked like. So two days later, bold as brass, I walked into the foyer of this impressive, huge BBC Manchester building and enquired after the girl in question.

"I'm afraid she's tied up in a meeting. Could you wait?" After over 10,000 miles of course I could wait.

Not long after a bloke who I recognised walked out of the lift, gave me the once over and introduced himself. I immediately shoved out my hand and said, "John Parrot, so nice to meet you."

He quickly recovered his composure to inform me his name was Eddie Hemmings and although he looked a dead ringer for him he apologised that he wasn't the famous snooker player!

"Bloody hell you look just like him," and he did and still does to this day.

He laughed at my comment and retorted as a return blow that I looked like Marlon Brando.

"Wow," I thought, "this bloke spins as much bullshit as me, he sounds like a good bloke."

Little did I know how things would work out, but after meeting the lady – who turned out to be very attractive – and delivering the package, it left me wondering what on earth she saw in my co-commentator. There's no accounting for taste!

Both Eddie and I never realised what was laying ahead for us both. We had a few drinks that night and we hit it off. Afterwards I wished him well and told him to give me a ring if he ever got the chance to go to Australia.

The following season my co-commentator and I were at the first game of the year at the old North Sydney ground where North Sydney were entertaining Balmain on the opening Saturday and both of us were looking forward to another exciting commentary.

Saturday was a difficult broadcast because of the racing from all over Australia which interrupted us at intervals because whilst rugby league is well supported in Sydney, having a 'punt' on the horses is inbred into Aussies. So often we had to listen to the 3.30 at Randwick and then pick up the commentary between each race.

During one of the lulls I noticed through my binoculars a rather attractive young lady and suggested to my colleague she looked a bit like that lady I met in England!

"You met her?" he enquired.

"Yes," was my reply and I also told him I had cheekily asked the lady what her flat looked like in Manchester.

It was supposed to be a joke to wind up my partner at the microphone. Little did I know he didn't take too kindly to such jokes and attacked me with both hands around my throat whilst shouting out: "You went to her flat you pommy b******?"

Fortunately the sound man was strong enough to shake him away from me and after some time he recovered his composure and we actually did call the game.

For some reason there was a bit of an edge between us for that entire season. Some people are so touchy!

I settled into the swing of things and the season was becoming a huge success. I was asked to move from radio to TV and work with the great Reg Gasnier, a man I respected as one of Australia's outstanding centres and a wonderful man with it – no edge and a dream to work with.

Alan Marks, one of the major commentators at ABC, also did some broadcasts with me and I started to get a feel for television while enjoying the game I love so much. I was keen to do my best to become established on the box but little did I know a few twists and turns awaited me in that area of work!

The job went well in my first couple of years at ABC and I was thrilled to be getting good comments from those in the media. Some of my comments didn't sit well with a number of the players, but I called it as I saw it and didn't pull any punches.

As a pommy who had played five seasons at Penrith I'd learned to handle such attacks from both other players and the media, especially the printed press who would seize on anything they could. The Sydney press have the same attitude to rugby league players as some of those in the British media have to well-paid footballers. They find the smallest thing and blow it out of all proportion!

I suffered badly when my first wife Patricia and my children Craig and Hayley went back to England and the Sydney press had a ball. It was often hard for any British people coming out to Australia in the early 70s – especially women – and we struggled to settle. It's easier now but way back then Australia was a real man's world and pubs and clubs had special snugs or separate rooms where women were not allowed! Imagine that being the case these days.

Time moves on of course and I settled down and got married again – to an Aussie this time – and Maureen proudly presented me with two wonderful girls in Kayley and Alyssa, so things were going along swimmingly.

Maureen and I opened a restaurant and it was going OK, so with my columns at the *Sun* newspaper and the ABC TV work we were sitting pretty. So much so that I decided to fly back to England in time to watch the 1990 Wembley Final between Wigan and Warrington and hopefully meet up with Eddie again.

I had arranged a ticket through John Huxley, one of the top men in the media, who ran the *Rugby Leaguer* Magazine in which I was writing a weekly column. Huxley agreed to leave me a ticket at the reception of the Sherlock Holmes hotel in London's Baker Street.

I was cutting it fine as I'd only arrived that Saturday morning of the game and rushed from Heathrow to the hotel only to find out the ticket hadn't been left at reception. By this time it was midday and I was beginning to panic over what to do. This was well before we all had mobile phones and I had no idea how to contact John who had set off for Wembley earlier that morning.

I dumped my bags at the hotel behind reception and took a tube to Wembley Park, still having no idea how I could get a ticket.

Fortunately I had my Australian Journalist Association Press Union card and I was hoping I could talk my way into Wembley. Not an easy task! Boldly, I walked into the general office at the old stadium and told them my problem but they were quick to say they couldn't help as I wasn't on the press list. However, after much discussion, I convinced one of the staff to take me to security who told me in no uncertain terms I had as much chance as meeting the Queen!

I told my story to three different staff before I met up with the guy on the reception for the top brass area. He amazingly said that if I had got so far then I must be important so he showed me to the press area on the upper level of the stadium. I was in at last, just as the players were running to their positions. A rather bemused John Huxley shouted out asking why I was late and nearly missing the kick off before he realised he still had my bloody ticket in his coat pocket!

Wigan – as they were doing in those days – ran away with the game, but it gave me chance to meet up with Eddie after the match and he introduced me to an Aussie bloke named Nev Smith who hailed from my neck of the woods in the Manly area. Nev looked like Dennis the Menace, the character from *The Beano*, with his curly black hair.

We struck up such a rapport that both of us left Eddie to explore the highlights – and a few lowlights – of Soho and to say we had a good time is an understatement. Nev allowed me into his workplace the following Monday to use the phone to ring Australia and talk to my family, saving lots of money which pleased me no end (a Yorkshireman never refuses a bargain).

Before I left, like I did with Eddie, I gave him my number and told him to call me if they ever they needed a commentator.

2

Eddie: The Ugly One

The phone rang in the office of BBC Radio Sport in the now demolished New Broadcasting House in Oxford Road, Manchester that morning. I didn't know it at the time but it was a call that would change my life.

I'd worked for the BBC for close on 20 years, first as a reporter with Radio Merseyside in Liverpool which turned out to be my dream job at the time. I'd roamed Europe with the great Liverpool team of the 70s. From Tbilisi in the Soviet Union to the European Cup Finals of 1977 and beyond – watching them win trophy after trophy. For a lad who'd once stood on the Spion Kop behind the goal at Anfield, this was Utopia.

But when that call came I had moved to Manchester and was the north of England outside broadcast producer for BBC Network Radio. Older readers will remember that in those days we brought *Sport on Two* to the nation every Saturday afternoon. The cream of the commentator crop was there – Peter Jones, Maurice Eddleston, Bryon Butler (football) Brian Johnson, Henry Blofeld (cricket) and Peter Bromley (horse racing). I was working and learning from them all. Some of the greatest voices ever to be heard on the airwaves.

It was a grand sounding job. The title said it all. It was my role to make sure, first, that the technical side of the broadcast from the football grounds, rugby grounds, race tracks and cricket grounds in the north was all in order and ready to go come 12.30 on a Saturday afternoon. Reporters needed to be commissioned, broadcast engineers informed – in other words the whole box of dice. All very impressive.

On match days I had to make sure the commentators were looked after, that they had the tools to do their job and that they were treated royally on the day. Seats secured, telephones ordered, broadcast lines booked so the world – yes we went out on the BBC's World Service too – could listen to their dulcet tones. With throats and voices suitably oiled the whole thing would run like clockwork.

If I'm honest the major work was done pre-match. Come the day itself it was all about looking after the 'stars'. Water on hot days, hot drinks when it turned cold – and of course it did turn cold on a regular basis during the winter. And this was part of the job I didn't like. I wanted to be in front of the microphone too not behind it. I didn't want to be the can-lad making the tea and coffee or doing the 'Bovril Run' as I named it. I wouldn't say I was looking for a way out. People didn't leave the BBC – after all it was a job for life. I just wanted to be doing what I believed I did best: performing in front of the microphone. That was the life for me.

The summer immediately before that phone call I'd assisted producing at Test matches during the Ashes series between England and Australia. The first Test was at Headingley, Leeds – we won by five wickets in mid-June. By the time the circus returned to the north at the beginning of August the series was all square. One-all, with a draw in the third at Trent Bridge. It was all to play for at Old Trafford and we were enjoying the cut and thrust of another thrilling series.

It was that summer I first came into contact with a man

who would prove to be the link between me and Mike 'Stevo' Stephenson. He was a cricket commentator with the ABC Radio network in Australia, a nice bloke who also shared my recently found love affair with rugby league as he was the commentator on league during the Aussie winter.

I had just embarked on my new assignment as the rugby league caller for *Sport on Two*, having on a hot afternoon in May, sat alongside Welsh rugby legend David Watkins – my co commentator – to bring the Challenge Cup Final between Wigan and Hull into the living rooms and on to the car radios of the nation. We had a few things in common.

It transpired that my Aussie pal had taken a bit of a fancy to one of the young ladies working in our office in Manchester. Neither of them was married at the time – so fair enough. But when the series ended that summer and England had won the Ashes by a margin of three Tests to one, little did I know that a request to a guy I'd never previously heard of would lead to such a career and life changing moment for me.

The phone rang three times. "Is that Radio Sport?" came the question from front of house security, four floors below.

"Yes," I said. "Eddie Hemmings speaking."

"Well there's a bloke down here who says he has a package to deliver from a commentator in Australia and he wants to see you."

"Who the hell is this?" I thought to myself. "Ok tell him I'll be down in a minute or two."

I finished whatever highly important task I was doing and headed down in the lift. The doors opened and I looked around. "There he is, over there," said the security man. "The ugly one sitting in the front window. Says his name is Stephenson, Mike Stephenson. Looks a bit menacing to me. I'll keep an eye on you."

So with heart beating slightly quicker than it had

been earlier that morning I strode across the foyer, hand outstretched and introduced myself.

"It's John Parrott!" came the voice as my hand was shaken by a man who had sausages for fingers, a slightly bent and broken nose and a smile as wide as anything I had ever seen.

"If I'm John Parrott you must be a slightly older and balding version of Marlon Brando then!" was my riposte. It didn't go down well! But this 'Australian' with … could that be a faint Yorkshire twang? started brandishing a bent and battered envelope, telling me he'd been given a package and had decided that, rather than just putting it in the post and risking it being lost somewhere between Manchester and Dewsbury where he was staying, he'd deliver it himself.

"You'd better come up then," I said as I shot a glance at the security man. Did I hear a sharp intake of breath from my minder?

"Please yourself," he whispered under his breath. "You're on your own up there. But if you need us dial the emergency number!"

So up we went to the office that was the home of BBC Radio Sport's northern branch. There was only me there. The others were at a meeting. "You could have a long wait," I said. "Why don't you just leave this with me and I'll hand it on when the meeting is over?"

"Nah I'll wait," said Marlon. "Anywhere we could go for a drink while we hang about? Looks like a nice pub across the road."

I didn't know what his definition of nice really was at the time, so suggested instead we head down to the BBC Club and if things really lingered on, we could always have a spot of lunch. Marlon was on his feet and heading for the door faster than the speed of light. Funnily enough when we got to the bar I was the one in front and leading the way to the pumps! It turned out to be the first of many encounters like this I was to have over the course of the next 25 years!

We spent a couple of hours chatting and swapping stories and I found out that this 'Marlon' bloke was in fact called Mike Stephenson – "Call me Stevo mate, everybody does" – and I also told him who I was … and who I still am! Turned out he'd played for Dewsbury in the 70s (I asked mischievously whether rugby league was actually played way back then). We've often joked since that the 70s are B.E. (Before Eddie) a reference to the fact I didn't get involved in the game until the 80s!

But I found him a fascinating, endearing character who loved to tell a good tale – many of them a good distance from the truth I bet – but basically we got on a like a house on fire. He lived in Sydney to the north of the City where that Aussie soap *Home and Away* was produced. If ever I went over – which seemed highly unlikely at the time – I should look him and his family up. Yeah right, I had as much chance of going to Australia back then as flying to the moon!

Eventually the lady in question returned from her meeting. We were back in the office by now and my new best friend, Stevo, was refusing to leave the premises until the package was opened. A thought entered my head; should I ring my mate on Security to get him out? I put that to the back of my mind and minutes later he'd talked her round. She ripped open the envelope and a return air ticket to Australia from Manchester fell out. Stevo's pal had invited her over to see how she liked the place!

I don't know to this day whether the tickets were ever used, returned, cashed in or even refunded. It's none of anyone's business really. But anyway Stevo's curiosity was assuaged and he took his leave of us with the words, "Don't forget if ever you're in Oz get in touch … better still if you're coming over for work keep me in mind. You never know we might be able to do each other a favour."

With that it was back in the lift and Stevo headed home across the Pennines a happy man.

Nice bloke, I thought to myself, shame I'll probably never see him again.

How wrong can you be!

3

Eddie: A Change of Direction

After the lift doors closed that autumn day in 1986 I returned to my production duties at New Broadcasting House in Manchester.

Following the 1985 Challenge Cup Final at Wembley between Hull and Wigan I had taken some annual leave and decided to join my long-time pal and brilliant football commentator, Alan Parry, on a two day trip to Brussels to see Liverpool in their European Cup Final against the Italian champions Juventus. Back in those days it was only the champions who were involved in the competition and Liverpool had made it to yet another final. I had been on official duty during Liverpool's run that year but with the final being on foreign soil I wasn't needed.

The Reds had taken on all comers and beaten them easily. Lech Poznan of Poland were disposed of in the first round. Benfica of Portugal followed in round two before Austria Vienna were brushed aside 5-2 in the quarter finals. The semi-final was even more one sided as Panathinaikos of Greece were humbled in a 5-nil aggregate score line – 4-nil at Anfield and 1-nil in the return in Athens. So the Mighty Reds – they were the best team in England by a country mile back then – were off to yet another European Cup Final, their fourth in eight years.

I remember travelling to Alan's place in Buckinghamshire

to spend the night before we set off for Belgium on the first car ferry the following day. There were three of us confirmed for the trip – me, AP and a pal of ours called Frank Jalland, but somehow Alan had got hold of a spare ticket for the big match and while we were in the pub that night eagerly looking forward to the adventure that was to follow – ending with the inevitable lifting of the European Cup again – we managed to persuade another of our pals, Mel Batty, to come along with us. It took a lot of 'persuading' let me tell you. Alan simply waved the ticket in his face, we had another pint, Mel went off to the loo to make room for some more of the falling down juice and he returned beaming from ear to ear. "I'm in," he said. "Too good an opportunity to turn down." No call to the wife, no call to his bosses – he'd call in sick the following day (and he wasn't like Alan and me – a bona fide Scouser!) but Mel was coming with us. Sadly neither Frank nor Mel is still with us but I remember the trip so well for so many reasons – some good, some bad and sadly many awful.

The next morning we were up with the larks and on our way to the ferry port at Dover, the plan being we'd stop off for a spot of lunch in Mons before getting to Brussels in good time for the kick off. It was a fabulous day, hot and sunny and we were in the best possible humour. Nothing could stop the Red Army returning from another final with that famous trophy safely in the bag.

It all went well until we arrived at Heysel stadium. The atmosphere was peculiar to say the least. But we made our way into the ground, found our seats and waited for the game to start. I can honestly say as we waited for the teams to emerge from the tunnel and on to the pitch we had no idea what was going on around us.

It later transpired that about an hour before the kick off a large group of Liverpool fans breached the fence separating them from a neutral area which contained mostly Juventus supporters. The Juve fans ran back on the terraces and away from the threat and towards a concrete retaining wall which collapsed under the weight. Fans already standing near the wall were crushed, many climbed over the wall and found safety but 39 others weren't so lucky. Others were badly injured, and as we heard the drone of helicopters overhead, only then did it become obvious that something dreadful had occurred.

There were announcements being made over the loudspeakers at the ground appealing for calm. I can honestly say that we never heard them. But when Phil Neal, the Liverpool skipper that night, walked across the pitch half an hour after the game was scheduled to start and tried to calm things down, it was pretty clear that unwanted history was being made.

The game by this time didn't matter really but the feeling was that it simply had to be played to stop any further trouble. For the record, Juventus won 1-nil thanks to a Michel Platini penalty. On any other day we would have disputed to a man whether it should have been awarded but on that night it didn't really matter.

The original plan was that after the game we would find a hotel, enjoy an evening in one of the bars in town and return to England bright the following afternoon. As we left the stadium and we saw what I believe were army trucks moving into position – yes that really did happen – we realised it was going to be Plan B. Bars were closed and the hotels shuttered down. We got to the car headed back towards Calais, sharing the driving between us, and slept what was left of the night on the dock before catching the dawn ferry home the following morning.

It was the horrors of that wretched night that did most to turn me off football for quite a while. I kept thinking to myself that I had watched one of the greatest sporting occasions at Wembley just a couple of weeks before – the Brett Kenny v Peter Sterling Wigan-Hull Challenge Cup Final. It was still fresh in my memory and over the following weeks influenced my decision that my future lay in the 13-a-side code. I've briefly flirted with football once or twice since but can honestly say that on a warm night in Brussels on the May 29th, 1985, my life and career changed for good. I was a rugby league man from there on in.

The Heysel Stadium disaster resulted in all English football clubs being placed under an indefinite ban by UEFA from European competitions. It was eventually lifted in the 1990-91 season but Liverpool had to serve a further three years in the European wilderness (it was later reduced to one). At that moment I confirmed that I would change career direction and the crusade to get rugby league recognised on a wider scale by a national audience began.

So in 1986 and 1987 I was at more rugby league games than ever before. In those days when the sport was played in winter there were County Cup Finals, John Player/Regal Trophy Finals and of course the good old Challenge Cup to go at. It was perfect for Radio Sport – 2.15 kick offs on a Saturday afternoon to fit in with the Grandstand schedules on BBC TV. David Watkins and I were at every one – my rugby league commentary career had taken off good style.

*****

In 1988 the Great Britain touring side was going to be heading off to Australia. I wondered whether the powers that be in London fancied sending me over for the tour. I put together the itinerary. The Test matches would be played early on a Saturday morning British time – Saturday afternoons down under. There would be three of them – two in Sydney, one in Brisbane – and in 1988, not having won the Ashes series since Frank Myler's team lifted the trophy in 1970, there was a belief we had a chance.

Ellery Hanley, Garry Schofield, Shaun Edwards, Andy Gregory, Martin Offiah and Mike Gregory were all on that Tour. All of them were world-class performers and Malcolm Reilly – a member of the 1970 Ashes winning side – was the coach. This time we were going down there to beat the Aussies and end all those years of heartbreak. The bosses at the BBC took the bait and I was on my way! Not with the official touring party though. Oh no that would be a bit pricey. Instead I headed out as a member of a supporters group tour and even though we would be staying miles away from the squad, my job would be to keep radio listeners back home informed – in other words 'do your best'. Commentate on the three Tests? Yes of course, plus the game in Auckland against the Kiwis as that was also a World Cup fixture. It was going to be the trip of my lifetime.

All I needed now was to find someone to sit alongside me and help me call the games. The Beeb was never ever going to pay for two of us (David and me) to fly half way across the world. Suddenly a light went on at the back of my head. I wonder whether that Stevo character would be around at that time of the year?

So I picked up the phone and dialled the number that somehow I found at the back of the drawer of my desk in the office. Now Stevo will tell you that when the phone rang, he was sitting by the edge of his swimming pool dipping his toes in the cooling water, enjoying a large gin and tonic as the sun went down. The fact of the matter is that by this time he was unemployed – and as I tease him mercilessly unemployable!

"Hi mate what's the deal?" he boomed down the line. I told him I'd be coming out for the Tests, that I needed someone with local knowledge to keep me informed and of course sit alongside me for the games and be my co-commentator.

"Any money in it?" came the inevitable response. "Yes a bit – but not much. This is the BBC," I told him. Without a moment's hesitation or haggling the deal was done. I'd be in Sydney the day before the first Test on June 11th at the Football Stadium. I'd ring him when I hit town.

Now I was staying at the top end (I like to think of it as the posh end) of the notorious Kings Cross district of Sydney. It was livelier at midnight than it was at midday. Perfect for a bunch of rugby league supporters of course but hardly the place for a 'good pro' like me to prepare for a Test match against Australia to be broadcast live from down under for the first time ever on BBC Network Radio. Yes, Stevo and I were going to be part of broadcasting history – well in our eyes we were anyway.

Needless to say I met him, we set to work and the partnership worked like a dream. OK we lost the first Test 17-6. We lost the second too at Lang Park in Brisbane 34-14. The series was gone. I wondered what repercussions there'd be when I got back home having told them in no uncertain terms this was going to be the year of the British Lion.

The fact that we'd lost in Brisbane though isn't exactly the abiding memory of that particular night. Stevo and I had to send a voice report preview back to London for transmission back home. We had to pick our way through the crowd to find our position – and even though the local fans didn't know me from Adam, they instantly recognised Stevo from his playing days with Penrith Panthers (they tell me he was quite a player in his day) and his time with *The Sun* newspaper in Australia plus his broadcasting on ABC Radio. Well, as we were about to start our piece to be sent back home to the Old Dart, things turned against us.

We were pelted with empty beer cans (they're as canny as Yorkshiremen in Brisbane!) and we were on the receiving end of tons of abuse from the terraces. "Stevo you bald pommy b******" was typical. It was the first of many similar encounters I would be involved in over the next 27 years!

In the week of the third Test things went from bad to worse. The British players were going down like nine pins. Remember this was a full blown tour, not just three Tests like we have today but a series of mid-week games against the likes of Western Division and, 48 hours later, the Presidents XIII – played just four days before the third and final Test against Australia – which was a World Cup fixture as well. The World Cup back then was played as a series over three seasons, on a league basis, home and away. The top two of Great Britain, Australia, New Zealand and Papua New Guinea would be meeting in the final. It was launched in July, 1985, with the final being staged in October, 1988. Ridiculous!

I'll never forget the final training session before that Sydney Test on July 9th at the Football Stadium. We had simply run out of numbers. Phil Ford was named at full back – his third position in three Tests on the tour. We had no hooker with Paul Groves failing a fitness test and his replacement Richie Eyres also missing out on his Test debut. So Widnes second row forward Paul Hulme played number nine and Hugh Waddell made his first Test appearance of the tour. Britain was getting savaged by the Aussie press who were never short of a word or two if they could bash the poms. The fact that we won 26-12 to end a run of 15 straight defeats against Australia and claim our first win on Aussie soil for 14 years, more than justified the decision to send us on the trip.

It was a fantastic match, Stevo and I were on our feet from first minute to last roaring the boys home, the first of many a joyous night we would have when faced with the mighty Kangaroos. Sadly one-off victories are quite frequent, never back-to-back wins but a joy to behold just the same. The sight of the great Wally Lewis being left in the wake of Martin Offiah as he launched Great Britain up the field with a surging run is the abiding memory. Martin's run culminated in a try for the late, great Mike Gregory. Wonderful memories. Great Britain had won against all the odds and we were off to party the Sydney night away.

The sponsors, Whitbread the brewers, had planned an end of tour bash at a swish hotel harbour side in Sydney. We sat down and the British boys came in to a chorus of Land of Hope and Glory – a swagger in their step. They had beaten the mighty Aussies in their own back yard at last, and stood top of the World Cup group ahead of the game against New Zealand scheduled for the following week in Christchurch. All was well in the world.

After the function we spilled out on to the terrace with, among others, David Howes who was the tour business manager and the coach Malcolm Reilly. The drinks were flowing, Britain had something to celebrate when suddenly the mood changed. Malcolm shouted, "Stevo – I'm going to have you!"

Now Malcolm isn't a man to tangle with even up to the present day. In 1988 he was at the height of his pomp. My heart missed a beat. How were we going to get out of this tricky situation? Malcolm promptly sat down at a table, rolled up his sleeves and the challenge was on. Mal fancied himself as a bit of a champion arm wrestler and wanted to prove a point to my new co-commentator. Stevo too isn't a man to back down. The gauntlet had been thrown. The challenge was taken up.

It seemed like ages before at last we had a winner. There'd been grunting, groaning, sweating and straining.

The pair had been destined for a draw but I looked at Stevo, and suddenly his arm crashed to the table top. "You're too good for me Malcolm," he said. Mr Reilly was delighted he had won. Personally I think that Stevo was getting thirsty and wanted another beer! Still it had been Malcolm's time so well done to him on his second victory in Sydney that famous day.

Soon after that Stevo and I headed off into the Sydney night. The plan was we'd have a couple more before heading our separate ways. Needless to say soon after I was abandoned in the middle of Kings Cross but at least my hotel wasn't too far away. I think we'd had two beers and I think we'd each bought one – though I can't be a hundred per cent sure! Anyway with a cheery wave of the hand he was off. He couldn't make the New Zealand Test the following week because of a prior arrangement so that was it.

When I got back home I got a message from Mike Lewis who was the head of our radio department back then and who had sanctioned the trip. "Well done on covering the tour. Sorry the result wasn't right apart from the third Test but the commentaries were brilliant and you've definitely unearthed a star in Mike Stephenson!"

The new star of Radio Two had given me a cheery wave that night in Sydney. I said it had been a pleasure working with him. Likewise, said Stevo, and before he abandoned me in the middle of Kings Cross on that Saturday night he said if ever he could help me in the future give him a ring.

"Will do," I said, but thought don't hold your breath. I won't be back this way again anytime soon!

4

Stevo: The Broadest Wigan Accent

The thought of working with Eddie left me excited and I looked forward to meeting the man with the big nose who looked like that Parrot snooker player at Sydney Airport. He looked somewhat rough after the long flight, appearing to have swallowed all the reds and both pink and black.

It's no joke doing the long flight from the UK to Sydney and I quickly arranged to meet up and have a drink at his hotel (I was certain he would have an open account to put on the bill for the BBC).

His hotel was in what we describe as the nice part of 'the Cross' – an area akin to Soho in London – and we enjoyed the lively atmosphere and a few drinks in the bars!

With Eddie not being from a rugby league background, I wondered if he would have enough knowledge about the game and its history to be able to do the commentary. However, I soon learned how much research and preparation he does – ever the consummate professional.

The three Tests were a challenge for the Great Britain squad and I wrote an article in my *Sun* newspaper column that it would surprise me if GB stopped the Aussies from doing a whitewash – something that many fellow Brits agreed with, and so it turned out in the first two Ashes matches. So nobody went into the final Test in Sydney with much hope given the Aussies had proved far too strong in the first two encounters. However, the last Test was a shock to Wally Lewis and all the other superstars in Oz who were confident of winning all three.

It was a wonderful day as a patched-up, out-of-sorts GB side took Australia to the cleaners. I have a great photo of Australian Captain Wally Lewis with the Ashes Trophy after that last Test and his face is all thunder. GB won fair and square and it wasn't a good day for King Wally.

I was fortunate to be available to work on the Tests because I was tied up with the ABC Broadcasting Company and they didn't have the contract for the Australia v GB series. So I was allowed to join up seeing it was the BBC in England asking for my services and not another Australian broadcaster.

To say Eddie and me fitted each other's style would be an understatement. We enjoyed working together and even the top brass at BBC Sport took notice. After the series, they even sent me a lovely letter (and a cheque) praising my style and saying how Eddie and I seemed to hit it off well. Amazingly the same bloke at the BBC who sent me the letter was to criticise my style many years later and suggested it really wasn't what was wanted or expected at the BBC! Snobbish or what? The reason I know this is because I had chance to read his letter of reply that was sent to a chairman of one of the top clubs in this country who had suggested the 'Beeb' should employ someone of the same ilk as yours truly!

Eddie of course was new to our game yet he demonstrated the passion that he has continually shown throughout our career together at Sky. I remember introducing the great Wigan stand off David Bolton to him in Sydney. David was one of the first English players to go and play In Australia in the early 60s. Eddie was so polite and tried to understand what David was saying, seeing Mr Bolton, who has lived in Sydney for 30 years, has the broadest Wigan accent you have ever heard.

"Who was that, Stevo?" Eddie asked after our chat with Dave.

"You've a lot to learn about our great game mate," I replied.

We had a great time in Sydney and I liked Eddie's style of broadcasting. He made it easy for me to be a colour commentator and fill in the whys and wherefores without shouting all over each other. It was a shame that I couldn't make the trip to New Zealand to finish off the tour but I was tied up with work for the ABC and the *Sydney Sun*. Eddie reckons the BBC wouldn't pay for my air fare, which was also true, but I had a contract and that was it. A few years later that wouldn't be the case, but more of that later.

Eddie has already talked about my arm wrestle with the great Malcolm Reilly which took place at a pub near where the GB squad were staying. Malcolm proved to be too strong even though I held him off for 15 minutes but eventually my right arm gave way. We shook hands after a strong contest which by this time had attracted quite a crowd including plenty of the press.

There were lots of British fans – men and women – and given the sponsor of the tour was a brewery it was a drinkathon from start to finish! One British female fan was a touch under the influence and somewhat loud in both voice and dress when one wag shouted for her to get her you know whatsits out. To everyone's surprise she did and the arm wrestle was soon forgotten as the talking point of the night changed. Then even more people joined the thronging crowd to the cheers of even more flesh being displayed.

It was time for Eddie and me to make a quick exit to a gentler environment.

Quite honestly I have little memory of what happened after that but I know I awoke in the hotel the next morning with a sore right arm and a tongue like a kipper-box lid.

I know the man who dyes his hair suggests I left him stranded somewhere outside a brothel which is not true ... I got lost myself!

5

Stevo: The Sack

After my Wembley visit and spending a few weeks with my children Craig and Hayley in Yorkshire, I returned to Sydney to find the economy was deteriorating. A depression was setting in which unfortunately was having a dire impact on my restaurant business.

I was losing money on the business so I decided to close it down. However, I took out all the pots, pans, plates and cutlery to start a catering company. The idea was that plenty of people can't afford to have a wedding or a party at a fancy hotel but with a catering service they could have the event in their local hall or in their own home and save money. Maureen and I made a good job of the business but it was taxing to say the least. Cooking, transporting tables, chairs, food and crockery was hard work but we made progress and we were getting back on to our feet.

Then the storm clouds really came over and within one week in March, 1988, I lost my two major earners when my ABC TV work ended and the *Sydney Sun* went bust. After 15 years writing for the newspaper and seven years broadcasting, it all caved in.

I sadly remember the *Sun* editor John Benaud standing up on the press floor and announcing that this would be the last edition of the *Sun* that would hit the streets. Simple as that. I think it was on the Wednesday and everyone at the

Fairfax organisation went into shock and typed out their last contribution to what was the pride of afternoon papers in the city.

Not surprisingly our competitor the *Sydney Mirror* was soon to follow but it was a sad day for us all.

It was such a shock that I never made it back home that night. Like most of the other staff at the paper I got drunk as a skunk in the famous Great Western pub and woke in the bar the following morning.

Fifteen years of hard work but great pleasure being a journo had come to a sorry end and it was well into Friday morning before I started to get over a huge hangover. Then to add insult to injury, a telegram arrived from the ABC.

My World Cup-winning mate Paul Charlton was staying with me at the time and was quick to say the messenger had said it was urgent. It certainly was urgent. They'd given me an offer I couldn't refuse … the sack!

It said: "Don't bother turning up on Saturday, your contract is terminated." Not a kiss my arse or anything. Blunt to say the least.

I quickly rang the ABC to speak to the rugby league editor and asked what was going on. He replied that a new structure had been brought into play and because of my English accent they said it offended the Aussie public and that they thought it better to have an Aussie in my place.

Amazingly it took them seven years to work that one out! It left me with a bitter taste and I demanded at least some severance pay but they refused to even to discuss it.

I made a quick call to my solicitor Colin Love, who would years later become the boss of Australian rugby league, and he advised me it wasn't worth the effort to take them on seeing as it would cost me more in legal fees than what I'd likely get out of a government backed organisation like the ABC. So I took it on the chin but I vowed that one day I would bounce back and show them that my style of broadcasting, with a pommy accent or not, would prove them wrong.

I later heard a rumour that it was the wife of one of the directors of ABC Sports who had said it wasn't a good thing to have an Englishman on Aussie TV. I do hope she suffers from ingrowing toenails and haemorrhoids!

So what next? Low on cash, low on pride and feeling like the world was against me, I went down to my local, the Royal Motor Yacht Cub on Pittwater, for a few beers with the lads to tell them about my troubles.

One thing I like about the Aussies is they don't have that stuffiness about them and they call a spade a shovel. They all laughed when I told them about it and bought me a drink. Before the night was out I had found another job ... digging holes in the ground ... and I started the following Monday with new industrial gloves and boots and a will to earn again, this time with brawn rather than brain.

6

Stevo: A Gamble

I thought I had hit the lowest point in my working life and even though I enjoyed working in the outdoor environment, it was a shock to the system to get involved in hard labour and not tap away at a typewriter. We were still getting the odd wedding and birthday party to cater for but the economy was slowing down in Australia and the country was hitting hard times with severe unemployment – something unheard of since the Second World War.

When you're down you have to change strategy and plan for the future to ensure there is food on the table for your family. Drilling holes was just about doing that for us and I was becoming a dab hand at icing a wedding cake, making pâté and even cooking to make a living. We were hoping the catering business would soon pick up, but it didn't.

Thankfully we hadn't spent all our savings and realised we could keep going for another six months or so but I was beginning to worry and then 'the' phone call arrived.

Despite long nose suggesting I was unemployed and unemployable, I WAS dipping my feet in our swimming pool when Maureen shouted: "It's that Eddie from pommyland on the phone."

It was short and sweet. "Stevo, its Eddie. A bloke called John Davis will ring you within a few minutes to ask you to come over and do the Aussie tour to England."

It amazed me because only a few weeks earlier I had started up a conversation with a travel agent to perhaps take a group of fans from Australia for the European tour and make some money that way. We even put out an advertisement in the Aussie rugby league press to see what response we would get. Evidently Eddie saw the ad and alerted John Davis who was Head of Sport at Eddie's new workplace at BSB TV Broadcasting.

After so many years at the Beeb, Eddie had taken a gamble and gone to satellite TV.

I spoke with John and it proved beneficial to me because he asked me what I would want to come back to England and join Eddie for the eight week tour.

At last I was being asked to go back into broadcasting. I was delighted with what John was offering me but it was only a short-term contract so I took a huge breath and asked for a bit more which he accepted and I was over the moon.

I know it was a gamble as he could have turned me down but I had to take into account the travelling all the way back to the UK. However, it worked out and here was my chance to get back into commentating on the best game in the world. I knew it was better than digging holes for a living!

Maureen and the kids were upset I had to leave them but I was only going to be a couple of months and I would be back home for Christmas. Even my wife admitted it was a chance I couldn't refuse, especially given the fact we needed the money.

That same evening we were invited to a birthday party at my mate Glenn's place around the corner. Late in the night I told Glenn about the trip. He was intrigued having never been to Europe, so I asked if he wanted to join me. I thought there was no way his girlfriend would approve of him being away for eight weeks but to my surprise she did. In fact she went away and came back with four shoeboxes full of money – fives, tens and 20 dollar notes – and after counting it out, told Glenn it would make him a better person to visit Europe ... with me of all people!

*****

I was excited about the trip which I had arranged to go via Hawaii, San Francisco and New York so I could have a few days relaxing instead of flying straight into London non-stop. I think Glenn only realised when we boarded the plane that he was heading to Honolulu!

I arranged the hotels so we had twin beds for the games and the rest of the time we stayed at Mum and Dad's place in Dewsbury. When we arrived in the UK we headed into the BSB building to sign the contract officially and walked into John Davis' office with shorts, T shirts and a touch of bronze on our faces from our round about trip. We quickly got down to business signing the official contract and I took my time looking over the eight pages before I spotted what I thought was a mistake.

When I had faxed back my intention to sign from Sydney I expected the agreed wage was for the week but this contract had per game! Having to broadcast two games a week doubled my contract money.

John looked puzzled whilst I read that paragraph over and over again. "Something wrong Stevo?" he asked. "No," I replied. "Just making sure it's all in order," and I left with a big cheesy grin on my face.

John was surprised at our attire seeing this was October in London but we soon started to pile on the layers when we went up North!

John could see no reason why Glenn couldn't be helpful on our travels, so it was good to know he fitted in well with the gang and acted like he was part of the crew.

I found John Davis to be a great man and he proved that in the many weeks ahead that we worked together. Although I was tense at times he helped me settle into the style of TV he wanted. He was a great boost for Eddie and me and he certainly knew how to put a television sports programme together.

I was more than pleased to learn that Nev Smith from our Wembley drinking bout had gone up the ladder and was John's assistant producer.

It was the start of something big. Could it get even bigger?

7

Eddie: A Gleaming Merc

After the Australian leg of the tour was complete in 1988 there was a World Cup match to be played in New Zealand.

It was the most convoluted World Cup tournament. Incredibly it stretched over three years and had begun way back in 1985! The nations – Australia, New Zealand, Great Britain, Papua New Guinea and France – would play each other on a home and away basis and the matches would be fitted into the international programme of three match Tests with one of the games being designated as the World Cup fixture.

I vividly remember Great Britain's first World Cup match in that series. It was a six-all draw against New Zealand at Elland Road, the home of Leeds United. In July, 1985, the Kiwis had beaten Australia 18-0 at Carlaw Park in Auckland, so they'd come over as hot favourites and very much the international team of the moment.

With time running out in the match GB trailed 4-6 when they were awarded a penalty on the right hand side of the field and Lee Crooks, the goal kicking prop forward, stepped up to take the kick. I was live on BBC Radio Two and I remember it was one of my more memorable pieces of commentary at the time. Nothing will ever rival the "Wide to West" try on Sky many years later but this one came close.

Lee was lining up the kick and I was positioned directly

behind him. It was a difficult chance to say the least and Lee was understandably taking his time. I was giving it my all: "This kick to level the Test against a team that has only recently beaten the mighty Kangaroos." It was a cold grey autumn afternoon as I recall and as Lee began the run up to take his shot at goal I remember saying: "So Lee Crooks takes in a few deep breaths of cold Yorkshire air ... and he's kicked it! Lee Crooks has drawn this Test match and rescued the series for Great Britain!"

In actual fact Britain had been deemed to have won the series because it was one win apiece plus that draw, so Great Britain as hosts, for some unknown reason, could clam the victory. I still get a shiver down my back when I think of that moment. It was one of the more memorable up to that time.

As a result of that draw and of our incredible win against the odds in the third Test at the Sydney Football Stadium the following week Britain had to head off for a one-off match against New Zealand in Christchurch for what in the end was a sudden death battle for the remaining spot in the final, Australia having already secured their place by this stage. Great Britain only needed another draw to make it. Remember, despite that win in Sydney the British boys were on their last legs. Could they get up one more time?

Now Stevo had told me before I set off for Australia that he wouldn't be able to make it to New Zealand for the game. I'm not sure why but perhaps as there were no expenses to be paid he might have had to dip into his wallet for his air fare across the Tasman Sea. I don't really know. What all that meant of course was that I had to find someone to fill in for the great man in Christchurch. And that man turned out to be Graeme West, the New Zealand Test international who was to go on and play for and coach Wigan in the years ahead.

I met Graeme at the stadium and we called the game. It was a tight affair and if memory serves – and I sound like a typical rugby league fan here – we were on the end of some questionable refereeing decisions from the Aussie whistle blower Mick Stone. Oh for the Video Referee that was to come in at the start of the Super League era some eight years later!

Needless to say we lost the game 10-12. Two tries from the Kiwi scrum half Gary Freeman cancelled out by tries from Widnes' David Hulme and Paul Loughlin of St Helens. 'Lockers' also kicked a single goal while Peter Brown of New Zealand kicked two, so we lost the match and missed out on the opportunity of playing the Aussies in the final that October.

For the record the Australians won the trophy that year 25-12 at Eden Park in front of over 45,000 people. Wally Lewis, Allan Langer, Gavin Miller, Wayne Pearce and company were too good for a New Zealand side that had the Iro brothers Tony and Kevin, Dean Bell, Kurt Sorensen and Adrian Shelford among others in their ranks.

So for me come July 17th, 1988, the tour and the adventure was over. I'd met and worked with a great bloke in Stevo, had seen yet another country in New Zealand and had a thoroughly enjoyable time. The win in Sydney and Stevo's arm wrestle with Malcolm Reilly were two of the many highlights!

Now I didn't head directly back to Blighty. Being out there for the Tour I thought it would be an opportunity too good to miss, so the plan was to fly my wife Carole and our son Mark out there for a holiday and take a while enjoying some of the sights of Australia. "When the family gets over we must get together," I remember Stevo saying. Actually we were only in Sydney for about three days – and they were three busy days and nights – so we never did.

I met the family at Sydney airport and spent a few weeks wandering round the country visiting the sights in Sydney first, heading up to the Great Barrier Reef for a spot of snorkelling and having fun before flying home via Penang in Malaysia where we took in some much needed sunshine. It was a wonderful holiday.

So I eventually landed back in Manchester sometime in the middle of August just before the new football and rugby league seasons were about to start. I remember someone saying that something called satellite television was on the horizon. Being a good BBC man I didn't give it a second thought.

Around about this time I got the chance to join a new sports programme which was about to hit the TV screen in the North West of England. I always thought it very odd that in a sports daft area like ours there wasn't a dedicated programme devoted to local sport. Obviously that was also the feeling of others and under the production of the late Ron Gubba, *Sportsround* was born. Eamonn Holmes was the presenter, the late Sid Waddell the reporter and the great Denis Law was the football pundit. I got a place on the team too and was the football and rugby league reporter and was actually given the task of presenting the news and reports in the studio. I knew I had good contacts at the football clubs but it was actually good old rugby league that gave me this chance. What a great game it is!

*****

As with anything new the six months I worked on *Sportsround* has to go down as one of the best things I ever did. It was wonderful fun. It was a great team headed up by Ron, and with Eamonn, Sid and Denis for company, we had a ball.

Having had a taste of TV it was a tough ask for me to go back to radio and my old role. I always thought I had a face for radio – that never bothered me – but the glitter and glitz of the TV studio, the lights and the glamour, all be-it on a regional programme, I must confess it got to me.

So I did my best to find a way in full-time. Thanks to a guy called Steve Ireland, who was the Regional Head of Programmes in the North West at the time, I was eventually offered a 12-month contract after I had badgered the life out of him. I would be based in the newsroom working primarily on *North West Tonight*, the news programme transmitted at 6.30 every evening, and when the second series of *Sportsround* came back I would be working full-time on that. I had been working, by this time, in radio for over 20 years on Radio Merseyside and then Network Radio. It was a big decision to give up my staff post and go on a short-term contract renewable every year with all the pitfalls that might bring. What would happen if my face didn't fit in a year, I kept thinking to myself. But the opportunity was such a good one I couldn't turn it down. I resigned my staff job and began work in the newsroom on contract early in 1989 – *Sportsround* would be back in the spring.

Then, one morning (around about April or May if memory serves) the phone went at home. A man called John Davis, who was a producer with an independent production company called Champion TV, was on the other end. He was setting up a team to work for Champion to provide the soon to be on air British Satellite Broadcasting (BSB) with the revolutionary 'Squarials' with the sport content for their new sports channel. John said he wanted me to be their rugby league commentator and presenter. Wow ... I'd never been head hunted in my life before. What a chance! But immediately I realised I'd be taking a huge risk in dumping over 20 years at the BBC.

Still I had to go and see them and talk it through didn't I? Well not quite then because there was a delay in actually getting the satellite up in the air! But John would be back to me as soon as possible and we'd arrange a meeting and sort things out. How long would it be? "Not too long," I was assured. "As soon as the 'bird flies' I'll get back to you."

The phone didn't ring for three months. I thought my chance had gone and it might have done apparently but for the intervention of my old mate Alan Parry. Clive Tyldesley, the highly regarded football commentator on ITV these days, was doing some rugby league commentary for Granada TV in Manchester on a new programme and John Davis had heard him and was pretty impressed. Alan was talking things over with John and John voiced the thought that maybe Clive was the one they wanted for rugby league after all. Alan dug in for me apparently and said in his opinion they should stick with Eddie. John listened, I got the call, and off to London I went to talk turkey.

I rocked up at the plush offices of BSB in London. I found my way there somehow and pressed the button for the lift to take me up to the offices on a floor above. The doors opened and to my horror standing there in front of me was none other than Nick Hunter the 'king' of BBC Sport in Manchester, the man who masterminded the snooker World Championships, *A Question of Sport*, World Darts. "Oh my God," I thought, "I've been rumbled. And the job's not even in the bag yet!"

"Hello," said Nick, "what the hell are you doing here?" I must confess I thought sod it I might as well tell the truth. It'll get out anyway. "Well," I said "I'm here to talk to BSB about joining them and doing the rugby league for them."

"I know," said Nick, "you're meeting with me." Apparently that weekend he'd been appointed as one of the top men at BSB and in a matter of hours had cleared his desk at the BBC and was now in London recruiting for the new company.

The interview didn't last long. I'd already made up my mind I was going, but it was also a huge risk for a bloke with a family to support. Satellite TV after all was the great experiment of the late 80s and there was no guarantee it would take off. We Brits didn't really like the idea of paying for our TV back then did we? Many still don't! But it's now seen as a necessity rather than a luxury. I had in the back of my mind that I'd go if they doubled my money and threw a nice car in for good measure. They didn't quite manage that but it was a two year deal and at the end of the first contract I would have, more or less, realised the dream. We shook hands and I was off home knowing I was about to join the satellite revolution.

The interview was held on a Friday and the letter of confirmation arrived the following week. I handed in my notice and was ready for a new chapter in my life. A couple of hours after resigning I got a call to talk with the Personnel Officer (Human Resources hadn't been invented back then). I opened the door and was asked where I was going. BSB I told them. "Oh ... satellite television. Are you sure?" came the reply. Well I was, I said, because they had made me an offer I couldn't refuse. "And would you mind telling me what this offer is?" I declined that particular invitation; it was after all no one else's business and I'm sure I wouldn't have been the subject of a bidding war for my services. The lady behind the desk nodded sagely "OK ... fair enough but you'll be back!"

Funnily enough I would never darken the BBC's doorstep again. I did have to work the notice period, though, and at the end of my last week I had to turn in on Saturday for the five minute news opt out at the end of *Grandstand* on BBC1 and the national news soon after.

We had just moved into a new house in Warrington and on that final Saturday I was due to take delivery of my new BSB company car. I had no idea what it was going to be, I think the phrase on the contract was: "Commensurate with your position in the company". In all honesty I was expecting a Mini. Imagine how I felt then when I answered the door that Saturday and there on the path was a gleaming white Mercedes Benz saloon. I thought I'd won the lottery. I drove into Manchester for that final shift feeling like a million dollars, did the show and then said goodbye to everyone I'd not seen on the Friday. Excited but apprehensive just the same, I was about to find out if there really was life outside the BBC. It was exhilarating but a little strange.

The following Tuesday I was off to London to really get to know my new colleagues. Champion TV was a branch of International Management Group, an organisation set up by American lawyer and sports agent, Mark McCormack, and based in Chiswick, west London. They were housed in a brand new purpose built TV studio. We didn't have any programmes to transmit yet – the launch date was March, 1990, but there was plenty to do in setting things up, getting a team together and talking excitedly about our vision of the future.

As I drove into the car park that day I was feeling pretty good about life. I'd be 40 the following February and I agreed with the old saying that life begins at 40. I was met by the company's finance man, a guy called Nick Meffey. His eyebrows raised as I pulled into the car park and stepped out of my gleaming new Merc.

"Who's given you that?" he enquired.

"The man who delivered it from the leasing company," I said proudly. "Didn't have anything else and they say I've got this for the duration."

He turned away and muttered something like, "Don't think you can have that."

I ignored this completely but a few hours later I was crestfallen to see a low loader taking my prized Merc away. I drove home in a Ford Sierra – a worthy but not very glamorous car to say the least!

Suddenly I knew my place. "Commensurate with your position in the company," seven words that have haunted me ever since!

8

Eddie: A Hundred Quid

So in the winter of 1989 I'd left 20-odd years behind me at the BBC and had jumped ship to join the satellite revolution.

It was time to meet my new colleagues. John Davis and Nick Hunter I had met before of course, but who else would I find in my new life? In those early days it was what you'd probably describe as a skeleton staff, after all despite the fact that the satellite was up in the air there were no programmes to do yet. It was all very much in the planning stage. People had to be recruited, some like me on a contract, others on the staff of the new fledgling company. Others had to be tapped up to work on an ad-hoc basis, contributing to programmes as and when they came along.

That first day I entered the new offices on the Great West Road in Chiswick with a beating heart and bated breath. It was a small sea of faces when suddenly I noticed someone I had met previously in my other life. Sitting at a desk was a little curly haired Aussie – none other than Neville Smith. Nev and I had worked together on one of his projects before, so at least there was a friendly face to latch on to.

Nev was, back in the day, a brilliant cameraman. He had worked for several of the major TV companies down under and in the late 80s (as all Aussies seem to do) had got itchy feet and had decided to come across to the UK on a six month working holiday to see what opportunities there might be over here. I think he too had heard that satellite television was about to be launched. So he packed his bags, leaving family behind 10,000 miles away, to try his luck in the big wide wonderful world of British TV. After all, and with all due respect, we in the UK lead the field in television round the globe. Standards of production here are better, I believe, than anywhere else you could name.

I had come across Nev some months previously. He was a rugby league nut and was sure that he could help to raise the standards of television coverage of the game in the UK if given the chance. He was a cameraman first and foremost but had fantastic production ideas too. All he needed was some organisation somewhere or other to give him the opportunity to deliver his skills and ideas.

He had been in the UK for a few months when he fastened on to the idea that there was a documentary to be made about all the great Australian rugby league players and coaches who were plying their trade over here. Men like Gavin Miller at Hull Kingston Rovers, Andrew Ettingshausen and Cliff Lyons at Leeds and Paul "Fatty" Vautin at St Helens come readily to mind. He couldn't persuade any TV company to take it on, though, so the only way he could get his documentary made was to film it, edit it and pay for it himself.

I can sympathise with the BBC and ITV of the day for not taking up Nev's idea, to be fair. It was, back then, a sport only shown on an irregular basis by the BBC during the Challenge Cup and John Player/Regal Trophy campaigns and, only latterly regionally, by Yorkshire TV in Leeds and Granada TV in Manchester when it came to the old first division. So it wasn't exactly a seller's market.

Undeterred, Nev decided to dig into his bank balance and do it himself. He would be the cameraman to shoot the footage and produce and edit the material but he needed a reporter to conduct the interviews and then someone to voice it in the final stages of production. He turned to the renowned rugby league journalist Dave Hadfield to do the interviews and somehow he'd got hold of my name (it later emerged that David Oxley Head of the Rugby League at the time had mentioned me) and he wanted me to do the voicing.

"There's money in it," he said when we talked on the phone. "I'll be recording it at Granada Studios in Manchester. It'll only take you a couple of hours and I'll give you a hundred quid!"

I thought a hundred pounds? I've got the last of the big spenders here! I tried to haggle and see if there was any more money in the pot. "Nah," came the reply, "I'm over budget already, can't afford any more. But I'd really like you to do it for me. You've come highly recommended." So highly recommended that I was worth £100! We've laughed about this many times since. Nev actually believes I was overpaid to this day. But I thought it must be a decent gig because, after all, it was being recorded at the renowned Granada TV Studios.

So I agreed to do the voice for him and we arranged to meet at the studios in Manchester where we would get the job done. I turned up at the appointed hour and noticed sitting on the marble steps of the building a scruffy little urchin who appeared to be scribbling away on a spiral bound reporters' notebook. "Good God," I thought, "didn't know it was this rough round here at this time of night. I'd better be on my guard. I could get mugged."

I turned the car engine off and stepped out into the dimly lit street. Imagine my horror and amazement when the scruffy little bloke on the steps rose to his feet, hand outstretched and enquired whether I was Eddie Hemmings. I said I was and we shook hands. "Neville Smith," he said.

"Thanks for coming. Follow me."

I went to take a step up towards the revolving door of the building as Nev took a step down and he ushered me towards the side entrance. I placed a hand firmly on the front of my buttoned up jacket just in case someone was lurking and was getting ready to go for my wallet! He ratta-tat tatted on the door and as it opened ajar a guy's head poked round, checked who we were and dragged us into the building before anyone could see us. What the hell have I come to was my immediate thought. It turned out that the bloke who opened the door was a lifelong pal of Nev's who was working at Granada at the time. Nev had persuaded him (another £100?) to allow us to use a facility inside the building to record my voice-over before they would piece the film together around it.

We went up the lift a couple of floors, came out and into an office which had a microphone on the table and a wire snaking away from it out of the door and into the adjacent room. "This it?" I asked incredulously. A TV set was brought in for me to watch the film, to get a feel of the thing and to try and fit the voice correctly to the pictures. I put a pair of headphones on, the play button was pressed and off we went. A few stops and starts later, less than the couple of hours to be fair, and it was all done. I left the room and looked around me. I was on what I can only describe as a balcony and looking down, there were all the sets from the soap opera *Coronation Street* below me!

It turned out that Nev's pal was working for Granada at the time and as a big favour to him had, very quietly you understand, agreed that Nev could use the facility to put the finishing touches to the documentary which by now had drained his bank balance down to virtually nil. It was a fabulous gesture when I come to think of it now. All very unofficial of course. No one at Granada would have known it had taken place – that is until now. Well, that's what friends are for aren't they? I've lost count since the number of times Nev and I have given people a leg up and a little bit of help. You do what you can to help people along in life don't you?

Anyway back to the night in question. Time for payment. Not the biggest pay day I've ever had to be fair but at least, I thought, a hundred quid in readies for a couple of hours work (Nev had written the scripts on his reporters note book by the way). So happy days. Imagine my face when Nev handed me his note book for me to write out my invoice and sign it as paid because he was giving me a cheque! I've said since that the £100 he gave me was the best money he's ever spent, and such a bargain too. He begs to differ of course and says I was overpriced. What he doesn't know is that I never did cash that cheque. I didn't want to get in lumber with the taxman you see!

So obviously I knew Nev when I walked into Champion's new TV offices that day. There were one or two others who were vaguely familiar but the great adventure had begun. As I said earlier, there were no programmes to produce, we weren't due to go on air until the following spring. So after a couple of days with my new colleagues I headed home and waited for the next assignment to come.

9

Eddie: Bold Stuff

So life at the BBC was over and a whole new chapter was about to open up at British Satellite Broadcasting. How much better could it get?

Obviously to be involved with something new and innovative was as exciting as it could possibly be. Remember this was something that had never been tried or tested in the UK before. Pay TV had been around in the United States for a long while and had been pretty successful. This was a whole new ball game for we British. Never before, licence fee apart of course, had we been asked to pay for our entertainment on the goggle box. So it really was new and uncharted territory.

British Satellite Broadcasting – BSB – had won the 15-year franchise to operate in December, 1986. The plan was that 400,000 homes would be equipped with its Squarial in the first year. It was an ambitious target but few of us believed, after we had signed on the dotted line, that it could fail.

However, shortly after the franchise win, Amstrad withdrew its backing believing it wasn't possible to sell a dish for £250. Australian businessman Alan Bond with others, though, joined the consortium. It looked like things would be OK.

In July, 1988, rival tycoon Rupert Murdoch, having failed to gain regulatory approval for his own satellite service and therefore failing to become part of BSB, announced that his pan-European TV channel – Sky– using the Astra system, would re-launch as a four channel UK-based service. The stage was set for a dramatic confrontation.

The Murdoch based Sky Channel went on air 13 months ahead of us at BSB. It was March, 1990, before we officially started transmitting programmes, though we had done numerous dummy runs, known in the trade as 'pilots', before we actually went live.

In the three or four months before we transmitted our first rugby league game from the old first division, there had been much planning and organising for what we believed would transform the coverage of the game in the UK and drag it kicking and screaming into the 20th century. One of the major innovations was to have a motorised buggy running up and down the sidelines following the play in close up to bring the drama of the runs, passes and tackles directly into the living rooms of our viewers.

It was bold stuff, the only problem was there wasn't enough room in most of the stadiums where the game was being played to allow for such ground-breaking coverage and technology. Add that to the fact that the game was then being played in winter and the surfaces weren't a patch on what they are today. So the buggy with its driver and cameraman perched on top kept slipping and sliding all over the place and getting bogged down in the mud. The idea was quickly ditched.

What we had to come up with was of course a commentary team to entertain and educate the population on what a great sport they were watching. I was the caller of the game but we needed someone to sit alongside me and add quality input into how and why things were going right or wrong. What made our plans so different though was the fact that the powers that be decided I would commentate on the games AND present the programme from either pitch side or studio. It was a move unique in broadcasting at the time. It was always felt that you had to have a front man holding things together in the studio who then handed over to the match commentator after the build-up and again at the end of each half.

I took that as a great compliment. I was to perform both roles. I would be the face and voice of the game on BSB. But before I got too full of myself I quickly realised it was a fantastic way of saving a salary for the company. One man two jobs – one man one pay packet. Brilliant! But I took it as a compliment to my broadcasting skills none the less and it is a role I have performed now for 26 years. Maybe I did do something right somewhere along the line?

My main man on BBC Radio, David Watkins, had already decided he didn't fancy jumping ship from Yorkshire Television who were doing a weekly programme of match highlights called *Scrumdown*. He was working on that with my old pal John Helm, a great broadcaster who strangely enough had also worked at the BBC in Manchester just before I moved in there. David was quite happy continuing in his role on the Yorkshire programme and I don't think honestly he wanted the hassle of travelling north from his home in South Wales on a regular basis (sometimes it would be as much as twice a week) or slogging across to London every now and again. So the hunt was on for my co-commentator.

In the intervening months on the pilots and then the first real live broadcasts we had used a number of candidates. Ex-St Helens scrum half Neil Holding was one, Terry Flanagan the former Oldham and Great Britain hooker was another. Kevin Ashcroft, the former Salford coach, had a go and even Gary Hetherington, the Chief Executive of Leeds Rhinos sat alongside me once for a Yorkshire Cup Final at

Elland Road stadium. I must say they were all very good in their own right but we were unsure if, moving forward, we had hit the right blend.

I do know that when we went on air for the first time on April 4th, 1990, for the game between Wakefield Trinity and Wigan, that the man sitting alongside me was the then Hull FC coach and part-time summariser for Granada TV at the time, Brian Smith. Brian was excellent. He gave a wonderful insight into what was happening and why and how a move broke down or culminated in a try. We were comfortable working with each other and building up quite a rapport. But Brian had bigger fish to fry in the game. He was a coach first and foremost and an ambitious one at that. We all knew it wouldn't be long before he moved on, and of course he had his coaching commitments to Hull FC who were one of the top sides of the time, so when we were at the Boulevard or Hull were playing way from home he wouldn't be available. Good though he was, we all knew it would not be a lasting partnership.

*****

Back in the early 1990s rugby league was a winter sport. We only had to get through to the end of the season in mid-May and then we'd all come back again the following year, hopefully with a new face signed, sealed and delivered to work alongside me.

The good news kept on coming through that first year. In the April it was announced that BSB would be beaming the New Zealand-Great Britain Test series live from down under in a ground-breaking deal that saw the first ever live coverage of a summer tour of New Zealand in this country. Domestically then we shut down for the summer but there was still the Kiwi tour to keep us busy, and it was subsequently announced that we had also secured the rights to show every game live from the following autumn's Australian Kangaroo Tour to the UK. Another ground-breaking moment.

BSB would show all the mid-week club games live, and we would also have secondary rights (recorded highlights) of the three match Test series which would be shown live on the BBC. It was going to be big stuff for us – a real dish seller, an audience driver and quite a capture for a fledgling pay TV channel that was not yet properly established to be fair.

So we needed to hit the ground running at the start of that 1990-91 season. We were still tweaking our commentary plans. We were also kept busy during that summer with a two hour weekly programme of highlights from the Australian Rugby League – the first time the game was being shown from down under within days of the games being played the previous weekend.

It was busy, great fun and wonderful to be part of something new that really was being well received. Nev Smith was producing those ARL programmes and I was fronting them alongside again a number of co-presenters, but more often than not Terry Flanagan. We did the programme live from the Champion TV studios – about 10 o'clock on a Wednesday night if memory serves – and then we'd travel back home on the Thursday.

It was while I was in London one Wednesday, preparing for the programme, catching up with reports down under and scanning through the Aussie RL magazines, that I turned the page and took a sharp intake of breath. There was a photo in the middle of an advert for a supporters' trip which was coming to England for the 1990 Kangaroo Tour hosted by – yes you've guessed it – Stevo! A thought flashed through my mind. Could he possibly have time to leave his supporters and work with me again?

I took the magazine *Big League* in to John Davis's office and asked the question: "How about we employ Stevo for the Tour and see how we go? We worked together in 1988 and he was pretty well received over here." John's response was positive so I picked up the phone, dialled Sydney in Australia and set the ball rolling.

Looking back I was taking a huge gamble because at the time Stevo was something of a Jonah of the media in Australia! He'd just got the bullet from the *Sydney Sun*, ABC TV had decided his wasn't the accent they wanted on the air anymore, and his restaurant business had just gone down the gurgler too. Isn't it amazing when things like that happen – three doors slam in your face and then another one opens up in front of you?

Anyway John Davis made the call, the deal was done and a few weeks later Stevo was on his way over. The Eddie and Stevo partnership was about to be re-kindled.

10

Eddie: We're Doing the Game

So Stevo was on his way over. It was only a short-term gig – October 7th until November 24th – but it would be good to see him again and I was really looking forward to working alongside him once more.

I remember the day he first came into the office in Chiswick to finalise the contract vividly. Remember he'd just left the heat of an Australian spring behind him. But this was London in autumn. We were all shivering in the cold and Stevo bowled into the office looking like a beach bum from Bondi! Colourful shirt, shorts, sunglasses and trainers. I thought to myself: "Nice way to turn up for your first meeting with your new employers. This could be over before it begins!" He also had a pal of his alongside him, Glen Farrell, who he had somehow persuaded to come along for the ride!

Anyway I must have given him good billing because rather than show him the door, John Davis produced a contract and a pen and told Stevo to sign on the dotted line. It took him all of ten seconds to peruse the details of the document. The only thing that mattered of course was the bottom line, the money. You can take the lad out of Yorkshire but you can't take Yorkshire out of the lad! So with a grin and a swish of the pen, Stevo was on board.

The 1990, 13-match tour was to prove the most successful

since the 1963 visit by the Kangaroos. In 1963 the total attendance was almost 287,000 over 22 games, whereas in 1990, with nine fewer games, almost 260,000 turned out. The highlight was the first Test at Wembley Stadium. It was a bold move by the Rugby Football League and it was also controversial because it was taking the game's showpiece match out of the heartlands, especially as two previous attempts to stage Tests at Wembley had flopped miserably in 1963 and again in 1973. But on October 27th, 1990, a then British Test record crowd of over 54,000 turned up to witness Great Britain enter the stadium to the strains of Land of Hope and Glory and claim a dramatic 19-12 victory.

Of course the BBC had shown that game live; we at BSB had to be content with recorded highlights later that night. It's a game I'll never forget though. Ellery Hanley was the skipper and led from the front in magnificent style, and when the Hull winger Paul Eastwood went over for his second try of the game nine minutes from time, I uttered the words: "And surely now Great Britain have won this Test match." By God they had. I've uttered those words again a few times since, only to be left with egg on my face, but that day it was true. Britain had won a magnificent game.

It had taken a bit of an effort for us to get that far with any enthusiasm left, to be fair. The tour had started at Knowsley Road on November 7th with a game to mark the centenary celebrations of St Helens' famous old ground. It had been chosen because the great Mal Meninga, who had worn the St Helens red vee with pride on a short-term playing stint in 1985, was by now captain of the Kangaroos and would be making a sentimental return. There was nothing sentimental about it; the Australians ran in eight tries (big Mal scored two of them) and won by 34-4. When three days later, with the mid-week side on duty, they had beaten Wakefield 36-

18, and then another three days on had beaten the mighty Wigan 34-6 at Central Park, we were left wondering how on earth we could keep this going?

But keep on going we did, though by November 6th, and with a playing record of seven wins from eight to Australia, we turned up in Halifax not knowing whether we were in a job or not as by now it had been announced that BSB had been 'acquired' by Rupert Murdoch's Sky TV. BSB was to become known as British Sky Broadcasting. Redundancies had been announced in the company and we travelled over to Thrum Hall, the old Halifax ground, not really knowing if we were in a job or not and indeed whether we would go on air that night with the game as scheduled.

I had known I had taken a gamble leaving the BBC 12 months previously. My father-in-law, Joe, had warned me that people don't leave the BBC. It was after all a job for life. But it was something I wanted to do. I'd got this far – almost 12 months in – and was desperate for it to go on a lot longer.

We got to the ground that day and there was a nervous air about the place. Apparently there was a high powered meeting being held somewhere in London and at seven o'clock we would be receiving a phone call telling us either to pull the plug as it was all over, or crack on and do the game as planned. The minutes ticked by unbelievably slowly that day. Eventually the fateful hour arrived and we were all gathered around the door of the TV scanner waiting for the hot line to London to ring so that we would know our fate. At the allotted time, bang on the button, the telephone rang. John Davis answered it. "This is it Stevo," I whispered. "You'll be on the plane home tomorrow morning." John took the call, his face not showing a trace of emotion and then hung up. He took a deep breath and turned to us. "That was London," he said. "It's a go – we're doing the game."

The relief was incredible, we were still in gainful employment and about to do game nine of the tour. It subsequently turned out we had a real ally in our corner that night. David Hill had come across to Champion from Sky to run the new sports channel. He was a powerful figure in the Murdoch organisation. He was trusted implicitly and his judgement was rarely if ever questioned. Turns out David is a massive rugby league fan – what a time to have a genuine supporter of the code in your corner! We carried on that night and the rest, as they say, is history.

*****

It wasn't long before we met David Hill in the office in London. Stevo had been bragging that he knew the man he called 'Hilly' from his days at ABC in Australia. He was a great guy he assured us. He knew him well. We'll be OK. The morning that David Hill strode into his office in London when we were there for the first time, Stevo tried to prove his point.

As David went to close the door Stevo was on him in a flash. "David good to see you!" he beamed and they shook hands vigorously. "I was wondering whether you'd be free for lunch sometime soon. Be nice to catch up." Now remember Stevo was in the middle of a short-term contract. To all intents and purposes the Kangaroo Tour would end on November 24th and he would be on his way home to Australia for Christmas and who knew what.

David Hill looked at him somewhat incredulously. "Lunch?" he bellowed. "Look at this, (his diary) I've got a meeting with some of the most important people in the world coming up. Lords and Ladies, businessmen and investors. They're all lined up to meet me at some stage over the next few weeks. And you want ME to have lunch with YOU? Stevo, I don't have time to have lunch with hired hacks. Don't bother asking again!"

The lad slunk back to his desk. We all smiled sagely. A hired hack? Obviously he knew Stevo very well!

11

Stevo: Boots 'n' All

After the Kangaroo tour John Davis spoke to me and said: "We would love you to come back, you and Eddie have hit the high spots and we think we can make it a long run."

I was flattered but said I would have to think about it.

Then both Glenn and I decided to spend a few days in Tenerife to get a bit of sunshine before heading back home to Sydney. It turned out to be a good idea indeed and we both enjoyed the sun, fun and the food, a vice that is true to my heart … or should I say belly.

During that time relaxing I wondered about John's offer and coming back to England to finish the season off which ran until May the following year (remember these were the days when we played in the winter). Yes, it was a nice offer, but I had two young children and a wife in Sydney. It wasn't an easy decision to make, but finances were tight at home and the mortgage had to be paid somehow.

I decided I wouldn't give an answer until I had discussed it sensibly with my wife Maureen. But when I got home, we soon came to a decision when a pile of bills dropped through the letter box. So we decided there and then that I would go back to England to earn the money while they would stay at home and spend it! It still counts to this day and all three have made a fine job of keeping their word with spending, spending and even more spending.

So off I went back to England to re-start a career that not even Eddie and I could have envisaged would last so long – 26 years in fact – so in many ways I feel it's now the right time to retire and let someone step up into my shoes. It all seems to have gone so quickly but I can still remember those early days when it was tough cracking an audience and establishing the partnership that would hopefully leave a mark.

There have been lows and highs, but fortunately many more highs, and I'm proud to think Eddie and I, and the team at Sky, have done a good job at presenting rugby league. There have been times when we've endured heartache and criticism – some of it warranted – and there have been occasions when we've fallen out. But like any good friendship, we've got through the difficult times and laughed about them afterwards.

*****

Getting an audience to watch wasn't easy, especially when plenty of newspapers were keen to criticise Sky and the owner Rupert Murdoch. One major critic was an ex BBC boss who delighted in bagging the Sky product in his newspaper column. David Hill used to come out from his office each time the old codger had had a go, telling us all to keep at it and ignore such rubbish.

That wasn't easy and often at dinner parties or functions people would ask: "And what industry are you in?" I was quick to tell them I worked in the media for Rupert Murdoch's organisation at Sky, which often had them quickly changing the subject or heading off elsewhere.

Amazingly when the rugby league TV war was on between Murdoch and Packer over the launch of Super League, my children started being harassed by other kids at school because I worked for Mr Murdoch. It got so bad I had to sort it out with the teachers when I returned to Sydney. Not many people in England realise what a huge split it became down under, but I demanded the teachers put a stop to the bullying at school. Whether others liked what I did or not, it wasn't fair for them to take their grudges out on my kids.

After my first season, Hilly gave me another contract. This time for two years instead of one, which lifted my spirits. He also increased my wage structure which went a long way to making up for my absence away from my family.

Soon after, Sky also agreed a new contract with the RFL and that gave us exclusive rights to show games on what was now called British Sky Broadcasting. At this time we got our heads together to create a format for the future of rugby league on TV which included a weekly magazine style show – *Boots 'n' All* – to give more to the subscribers.

Eddie reckons that I copied the name *Boots 'n' All* from a TV show in New Zealand but I swear I didn't. Until he told me I didn't know there was a show of the same name in Auckland!

Of course by this time Nev Smith had become producer/ director and was not against listening to some of the most outrageous suggestions for what went out on *Boots 'n' All*. Nev had been pleading with Hilly for months to give us the show as we knew it would be a hit with the fans. It was and it lasted nearly 23 years. I reckon only the *Archers* and *Coronation Street* have lasted longer.

Nev eventually got permission for the show and though Eddie and David claimed they were the reason for getting it on air, I know full well it was Nev's idea first.

It was in those early days that we brought Ian Proctor on board. Ian has the most amazing knowledge of rugby league, nobody comes near him for facts and figures about the game. Without him we couldn't have brought you so much information whilst we broadcast the matches. Each week Ian produces a printed file which covers everything we want to know about the games we're covering. From information about the clubs to details about each player – cups won, number of games, points scored, internationals and more – you name it, Ian's got the information for us. So next time you hear Eddie spouting off about something, it's Ian Proctor's brain that's providing those lovely bits of knowledge!

Ian has been like a brother to us both and despite a lot of things changing at Sky these days, Ian and I still call in for a quick drink at a local pub after each game. It's a tradition I don't want to stop, even if it's for just one pint, as it's great for the camaraderie. In those early days the after-match pub sessions were a bit livelier, but times change, many have got married and have children and I guess the rest of us have mellowed as we've got older.

But in those early days we often went by the seats of our pants and we'd probably be reprimanded now for some of the things we said. Not that we swore or anything, but I remember getting an irate letter from a vicar in Wakefield who objected to me saying 'Jeez' when I was describing a great try or kick at goal. He said I was taking the Lord's name in vain. I wrote back explaining it was a common colloquialism in Australia but out of respect I stopped using it.

Sadly David departed for America after a quick call from Mr Murdoch who wanted to take on the giants of sport in in the USA. Within two hours of that call, he was boarding Concorde and flew to New York to set up what is now called Fox Sports where he became CEO.

Only days before Hilly left for the Big Apple he called me

into the office with his loud voice making everyone at their desks shudder. He was so loud they all knew I was in for a roasting.

"Close the door," he said, and my knees went weak.

"Sit down and tell me at least four good jokes that I can use at a speech that's just been dumped on me in the last hour."

Luckily I had a few left in the bank so reeled them off one by one.

"That's good … that's shite … yes that's a good one," and so on for at least ten minutes. He then told me to get out and leave the door wide open on my way back to my desk.

I was halfway there when he stormed out and bellowed out loud: "And Stevo, if you ever do that again you'll be on the first plane back to Sydney!"

To this day I haven't let on what I had supposedly done wrong, even after weeks of grilling from Eddie and Neville.

There was one occasion when I had every right to have been sacked. It occurred at the first Christmas party we had in the old building at Sky. They had brought in caterers, a bar and a disco with lights. Later in the evening I was standing with Hilly and two female members of the legal staff and I noticed all three had near empty wine glasses so I politely enquired if I could get them a refill.

"Why that would be kind," so off I went to ask the young barmaid for four glasses of white wine and told her I would be back soon as I rushed off to the toilet. On my return I was presented with four pint glasses full to the brim. "Sorry," she said. "We've run out of wine glasses, this is all we have." Obviously, she was new to the job.

I should have refused but the devil in me took the four tumblers to David and the two ladies. It didn't go down too well and all three disappeared quicker than a flash which left me with no option but to take my Mother's words of 'waste not, want not' on board. Quite right too and I drank all four within a short space of time.

Things went OK until they grabbed me to join the Hokey Cokey which decided to go up on to the stage where the disco was playing when I slipped and created a massive heap of people.

Someone described me later like a cockroach on its back desperately trying to right itself!

Nev saved me that night and persuaded the security guards not to throw me out into the street. He steered me into Hilly's office where I slept like a log until seven in the morning, giving me just enough time to escape before he arrived for work.

I sent David an apology later that day and he rang me saying, "No problems mate – grip of the grape. It gets us all from time to time."

It was an almighty grip I can tell you. I suffered for three days after and was thankful Mr Hill had a sense of humour.

12

Eddie: Cinderella

At the end of that 1990 Kangaroo Tour, Stevo did head back home. He had made an impression though. He was a straight talker and never afraid of giving his opinion. Just as in 1988 down under for the BBC, the chemistry between us had worked well. The question was would he come back again at the start of 1991 on a more long-term deal?

The telephone call was made and after a bit of wondering and a phone call or two with me about the future of satellite TV in the UK and whether we thought it really did have a future, a deal was done for him to return early in January to continue to work alongside me on our coverage of The Big League – the Stones Bitter Championship First Division.

We were still very much the new kids on the TV block but it was obvious that we had something going that could possibly stand the test of time. The dishes were selling and our coverage of rugby league was getting rave revues from those lucky enough to see it.

We got through to the end of that season. The biggest night we had in those first couple of months was the shoot out for the Championship at Central Park between the top two at the time, Wigan and Leeds (no Warriors or Rhinos had even been dreamt about then). The winners would play the following weekend needing a win to take the title.

It was such a big game that they'd actually decided

a "proper" presenter was needed for this one so John Inverdale was despatched north to present the show while I took my place in the commentary box.

Ex-Great Britain Coach Maurice Bamford was a good pal of mine in those days and we got him to be the studio guest alongside John. Such was the crush of people trying to get into the game the kick off had to be delayed by a quarter of an hour. John and Maurice did a sterling job filling in from the studio before handing over to me for the game. The match turned out to be an absolute thriller as matches between Wigan and Leeds invariably are. It was breathless from start to finish.

However, one thing that galled all of us was the fact that the following match – when Wigan went on to lift the old Championship trophy in front of another full house at Central Park – was shown on Granada TV that day. BSB and Granada were sharing the rights to broadcast the Championship that year. That weekend they had first pick. We had shown every game up to the last one that mattered and it was taken away from us because of a clause in the TV contract. I still wonder now whether that was the day that it was decided we had to get exclusive rights in the rugby league contract the next time it was renewed.

The main thing was we were up and running and indeed the TV contract with the RFL was to be renewed. Sky, as we were now called, or British Sky Broadcasting to maintain the link with the original company, played an ace card in the negotiations. A programme called *Boots 'n' All* had started in 1991 and the story behind how we got that on the air was quite amusing.

Neville Smith, who by now had been given the heady title of executive producer and director, had been virtually camped outside the office of David Hill for months. He had been pleading with him for over a year to get a magazine programme started to run alongside our match coverage. David had always given a blunt reply to all his pleadings. Nev had even taken to sending emails (the same one) every week or two. Still he got the same reply!

There was one afternoon I was in David's office. I think I was trying to negotiate a pay rise in actual fact and the venerable Mr Hill asked me what I thought we could do to improve our coverage and attract more viewers to the great game. "Quite simple," I said. "How about a magazine programme?" Imagine my amazement when he said what a great idea that was. He leapt for the door and bellowed down to the other end of the office, "Nevvo – get in here!"

Nev came wandering down looking bemused. And he was further perplexed a few moments later when he was told that David and me had been chatting and I'd come up with a cracking idea, we were going to do a magazine programme all about rugby league. His response was, "Great stuff, why hadn't I thought of that!" So *Boots 'n' All* was born.

*****

We credit Stevo with christening the show as *Boots 'n' All* (although we later discovered a rugby union magazine show of the same name in New Zealand) and about six weeks later it was on the air. The untold story of that time was that Sky was in negotiations with the RFL for an exclusive deal for Division One rights with live Friday nights (a true revolution). What swung the deal away from ITV in the shape of Granada's live offering was the launch and commitment to *Boots 'n' All*, which set the platform for the years that followed. Hilly gave us the chance and it happened.

When the odyssey came to an end in the autumn of 2015

we had messages from David Hill and Vic Wakeling, who succeeded Hilly as Head of Sport when the Fox America TV Channel and the NFL came a calling. Their tributes to, and memories of *Boots 'n' All* warm the cockles of your heart.

This from Hilly: "Your history is impeccable, the only thing you missed out was Eddie had been in my office for hours, holding his breath until he turned blue, and I gave in. Seriously, congratulations to everyone involved, especially you Nevvo and those Rocks of Gibraltar – Eddie and Stevo. Unbelievable job!"

And from Vic who was our boss for years afterwards in response to an email from Nev thanking all and sundry for their contributions over the years: "How on earth did this programme – and you – survive for so long? It was, of course, the team behind you. The team you built. Wonderful years in a sport which gave you support and encouragement. Congratulations to all for a truly significant contribution to the Sky Sports success story."

What's more *Boots 'n' All* lasted for the thick end of 23 years before, in 2015, the plug was pulled and the final episode went to air at the end of that season. The offerings that were available in the programme continue to be viewed – but in this digital age on laptop, computer and mobile phones. My, how times have changed!

Boots 'n' All was a great show. It was unique to British television and the game of rugby league, a dedicated hour of chat about the game and it was quite controversial in those early days. We had a segment called 'Stevo Sounds Off' where the man himself gave vent to his feelings about anything that was getting on his nerves in the game. And there was plenty – believe you me. He proffered new rules that should be introduced, so good I don't think a single one was ever adopted!

We had a 'Boss of the Day' feature where we asked

leading figures in the game what they would do to improve matters if they were running things. And it was here that Gary Hetherington, then of the Sheffield Eagles, first mooted a revolutionary switch to summer football. *Boots 'n' All*, and Gary of course, came up with the idea a good four years before Super League was introduced. It was ground-breaking and immense fun to be involved with.

In those days, of course, the game was still being played in the winter months and at Christmas we produced the *Boots 'n' All* pantomimes. The most memorable was Cinderella – with a twist. I was the one who played Prince Charming (of course), Stevo was one of the Ugly Sisters (of course) and in our version filmed one winter evening in the cabaret room at Wigan's Central Park ground, it was me who lost the slipper (or the size 12 golden trainer borrowed from our Basketball presenter!) as I was the one who had to leave for some reason as midnight was striking in the background.

Stevo and I were dancing, just like the happily married couple we were! The clock chimed in the background and I put a hand to my ear and said: "It's midnight. I have to go." Stevo held on firmly to my collar, "You can't leave now," he said. "I'm sorry, I have to," was my reply. And then came the classic line that had us all in stitches laughing: "You can't leave me now," he said. "You've been MAULING me all night!" I exited stage right leaving the slipper (or the boot as it was) behind me, just about managing to stop corpsing into a fit of laughter.

It was then up to the Ugly Sister to find the man who fitted the boot. What do they say about artistic licence? Anyway Stevo then entered all the studios and all the programmes looking for the man who fit the boot – footballers, presenters, rugby players and boxers all tried the boot on with Stevo in full Ugly sister costume – classic stuff!

I remember not long after this we were filming an episode

of the programme in the snow at Oldham's Watersheddings ground high up in the Pennines. The blizzard was coming down thick and fast. Stevo looked straight down the camera lens and appealed to Maurice Lindsay who was by now running the game as its recently appointed chief executive: "Come on Maurice, this is crackers. Get the game switched to summer – we can't go on playing in this." Twelve months later the impossible happened and Super League was formed in the spring of 1995. Stevo at last had got an idea through!

Boots 'n' All had played a part in getting Super League up and running and, as a preview to the first summer season in April, 1996, we decided that we'd film some places that League fans could visit such as local theme parks or attractions before going on to the game that night. Workington Town were founder members in 1996 so we went for a cruise on a boat on Lake Windermere. We also visited the Yorkshire Sculpture Park outside Wakefield, and Kirkstall Abbey in Leeds. I'm sure you get the idea.

As Paris Saint-Germain were to be members of that first season we also went across to Paris and took in some of the sights there – the Louvre, and the cathedral at Notre Dame. We did attract some unwanted attention when we were doing our closing link and asked the cameraman to lock the camera off in place, focus it on us, stuff his jacket up the back of his jersey and walk through the shot at the back of us aka the Hunchback of Notre Dame. The local Gendarmerie weren't too impressed by our antics and were moving menacingly towards us. We beat a hasty retreat. Had we been arrested, the headlines back home wouldn't have made pleasant reading.

We were also lucky enough to be invited out to dinner in Paris with the late, great Jacques Fouroux and the guys who were running the Paris club – two brothers who just happened to own one of the best restaurants in the city. Stevo and I gratefully accepted le Petite Corporal's invitation and we looked forward to enjoying the gastronomic delights that were to follow. It had been a master stroke by the Paris rugby league club to recruit Fouroux and get him on board. As a former rugby union great – captain and coach of the national side – his presence on the PSG board gave the new Super League club franchise credibility and gravitas.

We arrived at the restaurant in a Paris suburb and were introduced to our hosts and shown to our table. Now Stevo and I both have trouble mastering the English language, never mind French, so we sat next to each other on one side of the table. If you take a look at Stevo it's pretty obvious he loves his grub and he has a particular penchant for the best that French cuisine has to offer. The appetizers arrived, pâté de foie gras. I got a nudge in the ribs. "Eddie this is going to fabulous. Shove a slab of this on your plate and enjoy," he whispered.

I must confess it was delicious, absolutely wonderful. The second appetizer arrived, a huge block of brawn, made on the premises of course, with the very best possible ingredients. By now Stevo really was salivating! "Eddie, this stuff costs a fortune. There's a few quid's worth in there. Help yourself. You'll love it." I did as I was told. It was good but in my humble opinion not as good as the foie gras. Stevo, by my side was slurping his way into it. "Oh … um … beautiful … magnificent. Oh my goodness Eddie, this is costing a fortune." Then I heard him cough slightly, followed by a bit of a splutter and a few more ums and erms and sighs and eventually a plop.

He's spat something out into the palm of his hand, I thought. And so he had. It was a sheep's eye! It had withstood the blades of the local grinder, obviously, and had ended up right in the middle of Stevo's slice of brawn!

I looked down and gasped. He looked at me then leant behind me and dropped the offending eye into the pot that contained an aspidistra directly behind us.

"Something there to see you through the week," I said. Stevo ploughed on regardless. I must say it was a priceless moment in a wonderful culinary experience. What a shame PSG only lasted for two years!

But by far the best moment in the *Boots 'n' All* history came at Knowsley Safari Park which is just a few miles away from the St Helens, Widnes and Warrington grounds. We decided to do the links for one of our programmes from there and we were taken to some of the most interesting animal exhibits in the park. Stevo did the opening link leading an elephant by the trunk – two tons of animal flesh (the elephant not Stevo) and its feet were only inches away from his. The elephant was looking at him straight in the eye apparently and took a bit of a swerve towards him that could have proved really dangerous. Imagine opening up a brand new era of rugby league with one of your main presenters from the knee down in plaster?

Strangely it seemed to set the scene for the day because we were searching for a place to do the final link from and somebody suggested the emu enclosure. Now from minute one I thought we would be doing this from outside the fence. Not Stevo. They were such docile creatures he insisted on doing his lines from inside the fence, surrounded by two dozen really inquisitive birds.

It was chilly, really chilly, and Stevo had a maroon scarf around his neck to protect him from the wind. This seemed to be a magnet for the emus. One by one they were pecking at the scarf trying to pinch it from his neck. One in particular made several attempts to snatch the scarf, so much so that Stevo decided it would be wise to remove it and he gave it to Mark Smith the producer who was on site with us.

The camera kept rolling, slightly adjusting its angle to get a better shot, when suddenly the bird came right up behind Stevo's right hand side and dived in with the beak … not to peck at the now discarded scarf but instead to take a chunk out of his ear!

It was a January afternoon as I remember and the blood thins down in the cold. So when the bird came down with its beak on Stevo's ear the claret really flowed. I thought for a moment it'd done an Evander Holyfield on him and sliced through the ear completely. Thank God that wasn't the case but it had nipped him pretty hard none the less and the red stuff really was flowing. To his credit Stevo was laughing loudly saying the bird had taken a piece of his ear!

I couldn't move. "It's bleeding," I shrieked hysterically.

"Of course it's bloody bleeding," came the response. "The bloody thing's just taken a chunk out of my ear!"

I was by now howling with laughter while the camera was still rolling. Eventually I managed to regain some composure and said, "Well you wanted to be in there with them." Stevo just kept yelling: "Look at it. It's taken a bleedin' piece out of my ear." There were more bleeps to cover the expletives on that two minute piece of film than I've ever heard since. It has become a piece of Sky TV, rugby league and *Boots 'n' All* folklore.

The story that wasn't captured on film though was when I asked the keeper whether, in all seriousness, we should take the precaution of getting a tetanus jab just in case of infection. The keeper looked me straight in the eye and said: "Not a bad idea but do you know … I'm not sure which bird it was!"

A classic moment from a classic programme that ran for 23 years – quite a record.

13

Eddie: The Hog

We got our first taste of international rugby league when in 1990, still as the fledgling and soon to be replaced British Satellite Broadcasting, the deal was signed for us to bring in pictures of Great Britain's tour to New Zealand. It was the first ever live television contract to cover a summer tour away from home. We weren't going to travel to the Southern Hemisphere though to present and call the games. Instead we would provide the studio presentation from London and take the local television coverage. Obviously it was slanted towards the home side, but it was a first for the game again.

Live, world-class sport was – and still is – what Sky is all about. That 1990 squad was branded as no hopers on departure but they returned home as Test heroes. The squad had an average age of 23 and had been decimated by injuries so the likes of Ellery Hanley, Shaun Edwards and Andy Platt were missing as they set off for the first leg of the tour to Papua New Guinea and then on to New Zealand to face the Kiwis. But they recorded a first ever Test series win down under since 1979, beating New Zealand 2-1. Former Welsh rugby union legend Jonathan Davies announced himself on the league scene and graduated to star status in the 13-man code by coming home as top goal kicker and top point scorer on the tour.

The tour actually lost money off the field but having beaten the Kiwis in Palmerston North and Auckland before losing the third encounter in Christchurch, it had certainly been successful on the pitch. The pitifully small crowds though – less than 20,000 in total watching those three Tests – meant the tour lost thousands of pounds. But at least the international game was given wonderful credibility.

By the time Great Britain toured Australia in 1994, we at Sky were going great guns. I'd made a second trip down under with Stevo, Nev and a guy called Mark Wallace in 1991 for the Australian Grand Final between Canberra Raiders and Stevo's old club Penrith Panthers. We'd got there courtesy of Qantas who were sponsoring the Australian Rugby League programme and we were transmitting on a weekly basis with the best that the Aussie game had to offer. We had come up with an idea that we should run a competition for two viewers to join us for the Grand Final and someone had somehow persuaded the airline that we should fly out too and call the game for the folks back home!

Not only that, we were all down to fly business class to the other side of the world and back and stay in some of the best hotels in Sydney while we were there for the trip. I don't exactly know who did the deal but whoever it was demonstrated a stroke of genius. We flew out two full weeks before the Grand Final and attended the semi-finals at the Sydney Football Stadium to get acquainted with the players we would be calling in the game. It was chance to do a bit of homework before the big day itself.

We had an absolute ball. It started with a house party at Stevo's lovely home on the Northern Beaches of Sydney itself and then we came up with the idea that we should go and see Penrith train ahead of the big day. We never actually made it and ended up instead heading for Newcastle Races (totally the opposite direction) and a day out in the champagne bar at the course! En-route we dropped into Stevo's pal's house on the banks of a river for a spot of breakfast – bacon, eggs and all the trimmings, somehow produced on an outside barbeque while we sat in the hot tub in the garden, swilling down the first of many glasses of bubbly that day. Satellite television? It really was all glamour!

Having taken advantage of Stevo's mate 'Smacker's' incredible hospitality, it was off to the racecourse for yet more fun and games! Would you believe we never saw a single horse run? We settled ourselves down in the champagne bar at the course and never moved. But the afternoon did provide a truly memorable encounter for Stevo and one that he has never lived down.

There we were – Stevo, Mark and me (Nev was away visiting some of his relatives not having seen them for a few years) – enjoying the hospitality of whoever's bar it was. I never did actually find out. We just followed in Stevo's wake and wey hey, it was a case of Open Sesame … in we went. The lad really is a star in that part of the world. Mind you it's the same anywhere he goes. The doors open and the drinks flow, with his hand never dipping into his pocket of course!

It was between the second and third races as I recall and we were chatting in the corner, enjoying the champagne and the food that was also on offer, when suddenly from the far side of the room we heard a loud woman's voice: "Is that you Stevo? You pommy b******!" The whole room fell silent as this 'lady' tottered across in the highest high heels I have ever seen in my life, fag in hand and a hat with a big black flower sticking out of the top at a real jaunty angle. And tottering is the right word. The glass was full – half full by the time she reached us – the flower waving away from side to side and the lady herself wobbling just a bit.

As soon as he saw her Stevo gasped and said something like: "Oh bloody hell no. I'm off." But I put my thumb firmly into his jacket pocket. There was no way he could have gone anywhere with his jacket still intact – and I said: "You're going nowhere my old son. I want to meet this young lady!" Before the words were out of the corner of my mouth she was upon us.

"I've not seen you in bloody years Stevo. Where've you been? What's been going on you little shit?"

For the first time in my life I saw Stevo lost for words. He dragged a name somewhere out of the recesses of his mind and said: "Oh, er hello Janine. I'm here for the Grand Final on Sunday. Err … working in the UK on TV these days. Can I introduce you to a couple of my colleagues? This is Mark … Mark Wallace, one of our top producers. And this is Eddie Hemmings. We're going to be doing the match commentary together."

There was a long pause as Janine took a swig from her glass, a drag on her cigarette and looked us both up and down from top to toe. "Oh really," she snarled. "Nice to meet ya both. And ay … I hope you're a better kisser than him!" And she poked a finger in both our chests and glared menacingly at Stevo.

It was an uncomfortable moment or two before she turned on her heels and flounced off back to the other side of the room. "Good God Stevo," I said. "Who the hell is that?"

"Oh just someone I knew in a previous life," came the reply. "And do you know back then … that dress actually fitted her!"

I'm still not sure who or what she was but Janine is now a legend in the Stevo story as far as I am concerned.

*****

We overnighted in Newcastle after the races as there was no way any of the three of us could drive back. So the next morning we returned to Sydney to prepare for the big game that would be beamed back to the UK the following Sunday morning. Now because we felt we hadn't seen enough of either Penrith or Canberra, it was decided that on the Saturday night before the game we should get VHS copies of the teams in action (DVD's hadn't been invented way back then) and we should watch them in my hotel room to get ourselves fully acquainted with the men who'd be playing in Australia's biggest game of the year the following afternoon.

The plan was we'd go out early for a bite to eat then head back and watch the recordings of matches they'd played the previous week, make the notes and do some 'homework'. The plan was good to go. The problem started with the bite to eat! With Stevo it's never just 'a bite to eat'. It has to be washed down with a fine glass of white – preferably Sauvignon Blanc. And as we were in the land of some of the finest drops of white in the world, this was an occasion not to be missed. Two steaks and copious amounts of wine later we arrived back in my hotel room, plugged the machine in, placed the cassette in the slot and began watching the teams that would be in action less than 18 hours later.

The next thing I knew I woke up. Stevo was flat out next to me and it was well gone midnight! Of course there was no way he would be driving home now. The Australian drink driving laws are some of the toughest in the civilised world. So Stevo was staying the night. The only problem was there was only one bed. It was a massive king size to be fair, so there was room for two or three or four! So he jumped in one side, me the other, with the pillows carefully laid down the middle just in case! And we attempted to get some valuable shut eye before our big day.

I think I'd been asleep all of half an hour when I awoke with a start. There was something in the room making a terrible racket. It sounded like a hog or something from the other side of the bed. Having re-gathered my senses I soon realised the hog was Stevo rolling them – now roaring them – home. He is the loudest and longest snorer I have ever known. I pushed him, punched him, slapped him in the face. Nothing. I got up to put all the lights on. The hog just kept on roaring!

What the hell could I do? I went to the bathroom and plugged my ears with the cotton wool they leave in those vanity kits you can use and returned to my side of the bed. But the earplugs were little use against Stevo's onslaught. I covered my head with the pillow and eventually dropped-off about an hour later. It was one of the worst night's sleep of my life. Next thing I knew the blinds were drawn back and the sun streamed into the room. The hog was awake. "Morning top man!" he said. "Sleep well?"

"Sleep well?" I questioned. "Sleep well? I've never put a night in like it in my life. You don't half snore. Well I think it was a snore, it seemed to come from somewhere deep within. I've never heard anything like it …"

Just then the phone rang and it was Stevo's lovely wife Maureen asking if I had any idea where her old man was. "I'm sorry to say Maureen," I replied. "He's been here all night, bunking in with me. Our research into the Grand Final got a bit out of hand. He stayed the night with me here at the hotel. He's in the shower right now and I'll get him to ring you back when he emerges. Just one thing I've got to ask you though. How on earth do you live with all the snoring? It was like having an old wart hog in the bed next to me all night. I'm absolutely knackered."

"I bet you are," she said. "Why do you think when I see that Jumbo Jet heading off back to Britain with Mike on it for the start of another season I wave him off and say to myself: 'Off you go you little beauty'. I have a big smile on my face knowing I won't have to put up with that racket every night again for eight months or so!"

And there, dear reader, you have it. The recipe for a happy marriage Stevo style. He's not been home longer than a few months in any year since 1990. For the majority of the year, Maureen gets a good night's sleep and the rest of the time she puts up with the creature from the black lagoon. Then she gives him back to me! Thank God I've never had to sleep with him since – except for one night on tour in 1992 in Parkes, Australia – but that's another story.

14

Stevo: An Uncomfortable Re-acquaintance

With the surge of interest and more and more punters buying dishes, it seemed the whole Sky thing would work out fine, especially since we had secured the rights for the Premier League football matches. This proved to be a smart move by the top brass and there's little doubt that it helped launch Sky into more living rooms in the country. Not forgetting, of course, the many pubs and clubs showing matches on a big screen. This introduced the duo of Richard Keys and Andy Gray to our screens, and it was obvious the pair helped us all get better viewing figures, that and the fact that we were putting out games live.

Well, not always live. Sometimes we would go to a match and introduce it before the game and record the action on tape. We would then go to London and put the commentary on top whilst watching the replay. Not an easy task dumping your voice on to tape whilst watching the game on a screen a touch smaller than the average TV you have at home.

The studios at the time were small but they had a huge window through which you could see people walking past all the time. On one occasion Gray and Keys decided to bare their arses to the window in full view! It wasn't a lovely sight, especially Keys' who has the hairiest body in the world. In those days we were recording the commentary as live, so no stopping, coughing or laughing.

Recording live on a replay wasn't easy but it was great fun and it had the advantage at times to make you look good by stating perhaps a chip over the top would be a great idea to break down the defence, and of course seconds later that's what happened.

Live broadcasting is the bread and butter of TV, and of course on the football side Gray and Keys were becoming popular figures on screen. I got on more with Andy than Richard who I thought was always bringing our game down. He is talented yes, but I would think twice before inviting him to my barbecue.

I remember one of the few times Eddie was ill and couldn't make a game at Hull Kingston Rovers where they were playing Widnes. Keys had been drafted in to host the opening gambit from the live studio in the stand and his first comment to me was that the stadium hadn't changed much since the 1960s. He was a bit sheepish when I said it should have changed seeing the Rovers had moved to this new stadium only a couple of years earlier.

He then asked: "Stevo, Hull KR?" And off I went going through the team line up and where and how Rovers could win the game.

Then his second question: "Stevo, Widnes?" And I went through the same as before only for Widnes this time.

He never said another word after that!

Not surprisingly he never did another league game for us.

Despite my opinions, the two of them did a wonderful job in those early days when we were desperate to make a mark. The fans wanted more and more live sport and Sky was giving it to them, especially football which started to give us all at the company a huge buzz.

Eddie and I of course tagged along and to our surprise the league viewing figures started to rise too. And amazingly a review of viewers from all around the UK showed that 25 per cent of those watching rugby league were in fact coming from the south!

Such figures are the lifeblood of commentators. It was obvious that even football crazy supporters were happy to watch the 13-a-side game, especially on Friday nights. It was soon clear that all the top footballers who were resting up in hotels before their Saturday game were becoming avid rugby league fans.

*****

One of our first trips overseas was to Dublin in the land of 'the black stuff' for the Charity Shield game between Leeds and Wigan. We arrived the Friday before the game and settled nicely in a top hotel that wasn't too far away from the Royal Showground where the teams would do battle. In the evening all the crew went out for a nice evening meal which was followed by a night cap when we got back to the hotel.

As we walked into the bar a voice shouted out: "Hey lads, look its Eddie and Stevo!" Eddie and I were baffled at the thought of anyone recognising us anywhere, never mind in Dublin. As it turned out it was Liverpool FC's Assistant Coach Ronnie Moran, who invited us over to meet his star players including Michael Owen and Robbie Fowler. The players were eager to shake our hands and made it quite clear they were keen fans of our game! Liverpool were also playing a charity match as a build up to their season.

It was an eye opener, but it showed that the broadcasts were getting out to more and more fans, and even the superstars of English football.

Eddie of course knew a few of the lads in football from his days at the BBC Radio. He also knew Richard Keys who, with Andy Gray, was now creating a distinct style with an insight into games with new gadgets and gizmos. These gave the duo the ability to show the viewers a much more technical side to their sport, and Eddie and I and Producer Neville were eager to do the same with rugby league. Nev was determined we were not going to be left behind and was quick to obtain the necessary video clips and machines to show the viewers a more detailed insight into our sport.

Our first attempt was with the 'Electric Chalkboard' where a magnetic pencil could show the different lines of running and the areas where perhaps defences were looking weak – all extra information that hadn't been seen on TV before.

Most of the time it worked fine but occasionally it would just set off on its own and we'd finish up with a lot of squiggles on the screen that made yours truly look like a raving idiot.

These days of course we have the TV Touch Screen where the likes of Jon Wells explains, in even more detail, how a game has progressed or was won and lost. But in those early days it was me setting up the right clip whilst being on talkback to the technicians, and then chalking away whilst still calling the game. It was stressful and took its toll on our nerves but we got through it.

It wasn't long after the Gulf War that a new gizmo hit the screens where you could actually trace the flow of the ball or the players. It was obvious the idea had come from the equipment used to set up missile attacks during the war! It was an amazing piece of kit but we could only use it for the midweek show as it took ages to set up but we were, like all the other sports at Sky, keen to use it.

Probably the greatest piece of kit was the introduction of virtual reality where you could actually appear out of the back of the scrum, stop the action close up and explain why, where or when such and such a player was out of position. The easiest way to explain it is when you watch a presenter of the weather forecast who points north, south, west or east telling you where the rain will be. The truth is they can't see a thing, it's just a green empty wall!

Standing on the set for over four hours with nothing but a green wall behind you and trying to point or position yourself in the exact spot wasn't easy. Each move had to be recorded and if you were pointing one or two inches out of position then you had to do it all over again.

The end result looked great but it was a pain in the neck just to create a two minute clip for the show and it cost a fortune to produce!

I can remember the first one we ever did which involved the Australian touring side and it took over six hours to put together. Nev and Assistant Producer Mark Smith decided it would look good if I finished the piece off by hitting the jaw of a kangaroo – not a live one of course but someone inside a dummy roo. Enter stage left a certain Ben Proe whose name you will recognise through his calling the Challenge Cup games these days, but it was Ben's first day at work and he was chosen to be the 'live kangaroo'.

Nev and Mark wanted it to look good and suggested I lunged with my fist just past Ben 'Roo' Proe's chin. I made it look real all right, I misjudged the punch and knocked poor Ben to the floor where he lay in a daze.

It was one of my best shots ever, both on and off the field of play, and we got it on tape!

*****

After that Dublin trip we were keen to spread our wings even further and when we signed the contract for the Great Britain tour to New Zealand and Papua New Guinea, we were hoping instead of having pictures beamed in live from overseas we would one day get on that big bird and fly to Australasia. But the opportunity came sooner than expected.

We had started to show Australian games each week in the UK when plans were put in place to fly out with the crew to cover the Grand Final live – between my old club Penrith Panthers and Canberra Raiders. Then somebody came up with the idea of giving away a prize for two of our viewers to join us in Australia for the final with business class flights, hotels and game tickets all included!

The two winners of the competition were a lovely couple who invited us for a drink the Thursday before the Final and boy did they enjoy themselves! But it was obvious they were suffering from jet lag having only arrived the day before and they soon fell asleep on the sun loungers leaving Eddie and me to make a hasty retreat to our own rooms.

Sadly we never had chance to see them again such was the heavy schedule for their trip.

Amazingly we flew out two weeks before the Grand Final, giving us plenty of time to get to know the players and for me to settle into life back home for a few days.

Eddie has explained about meeting up with Janine, an old flame from my playing days who had me looking for the nearest exit, but Eddie wouldn't let me go and held on to my coat so hard you would have thought he was holding his wallet! The upshot was I couldn't get away and had to endure introducing this 'lady' to both Eddie and Mark Wallace, our assistant producer.

Eddie explains it quite well in his chapter but I couldn't believe what I was seeing. She had piled on so much weight since the last time I'd seen her, and quite frankly it was a case of too much meat, not enough bread. To top it all off she was full as a boot, drunk as a skunk and wearing a dress that 15 years ago fitted her, but not now!

The scene took place in the Members Bar at Newcastle Races and, having worked in sponsorship with Rothmans and their flagship brand Winfield Cigarettes, who were heavily involved with horse racing, most of the committee and the patrons knew me quite well. I swear blind the place went deadly quiet as she bellowed out: "Stevo, you pommy b******!"

Eddie also refers to an old mate of mine, Barry 'Smacka' Moore, a great bloke who made a fortune in Australia by bringing in cheap sewing machines from Sweden into the land down under.

Smacka was a great bloke and a bundle of laughs who could drink for Australia and probably win a gold medal in the process. His father was an amazing bloke too and was the trainer for the touring Lions during the 40s and 50s when the Ashes were up for grabs. It was normal in those days for the GB Lions touring Australasia not to bring a trainer or even a physio on tour; they chose Smacka's dad Bill to look after them instead.

The tales his dad offered were mind blowing, especially the antics that went on at the famous Olympic Hotel just across the road from the Sydney Cricket Ground.

One such tale involved the great, late Mick Sullivan who was not selected for the Test match at the SCG the following day. Mick decided because he wasn't playing on the Saturday that he'd set sail for a few beers on Friday night at the nearby South Sydney Leagues Club, which had by tradition offered free beers to the touring Lions.

Mick somehow wobbled his way back to the hotel just before the dawn was breaking only to find a note saying one of the lads had broken down at training and he was selected to play. It didn't bother Mick one iota. He played that day and played a blinder, though it's debateable if he knew what he was doing or where he was. Either way GB won the Test!

Smacka was a legend in his own right and had moved up to the Hunter Valley to live and retire in peace and was eager for me to bring the lads to his place on the Hunter River. He had a nice pad overlooking the water with a hot tub, barbecue in full flow and bottle after bottle of champagne.

Smacka loved flying over to the UK where he had many friends and when he travelled into Europe he carried a letter from his doctor stating he was a chronic alcoholic and would bring back duty free from France, about 50 bottles of wine at a time when you were allowed just two bottles. The letter stated it was his medicine and that he couldn't do without it!

Thankfully Mark was off the drink and was driving, so Eddie and I got stuck into the champers big time.

Neville hadn't joined us because he wanted to meet up with his parents in Sydney instead. Nev thought we had gone out to Penrith, which is in the opposite direction to Newcastle, but as they say what they don't know doesn't hurt.

By the time we dried off from the hot bubbles, the cold bubbles had us in a joyful mood and we sang our way towards the charming racetrack of Newcastle where a friendly welcome is always on the cards. Smacka was left at the gate trying to persuade us to stay all day and even Eddie was tempted but we had to do some 'work'.

In the past I had often worked in Newcastle for weeks on end doing promotional work and I knew that free entry and Members Bar tickets were waiting for us on the gate.

We had a great time apart from the shock of meeting Janine but even that drifted away as we took Newcastle by storm and painted the town red. I must say both Eddie and I weren't feeling too hot the following morning, and even Mark was feeling dog rough but for a different reason. Mark is a vegetarian but for some unknown reason he'd decided late the previous evening to buy a burger off one of the street vendors. It was a bad move and he was up all night 'hugging the porcelain wishing well', although I never heard a thing.

Neville was eager to hear how we had got on watching Penrith Panthers train before their big day at the Sydney Sports Stadium. "It went fine Nev, we are both ready big time for the Grand Final," I said. "But Mark's not so good. Think he's got a case of food poisoning!"

Seeing Mark in such a state gave out a big warning of never buy any food from a street vendor late at night. I did make the mistake of forgetting that ruling years later whilst attending the Dubai Sevens to watch the London Broncos who had entered a team out there. It was late and I needed food so I bought a beef burger. Hours later when I was having an 'out of stomach experience' I remembered there aren't many cows in Dubai. I still wonder what was in that burger!

It was an interesting trip to Australia and we both stayed at the Sydney Hotel to watch a video of the semi-finals to get even more acquainted with the players. We decided to have a meal first with a bottle of wine. Sadly both Eddie and I fell asleep about five minutes into watching the video of the game and slept like a log … well I know I did but Eddie swears that I snored so badly he didn't get a wink of shut eye.

He's pretty good at spreading rumours. In fact the best way to let everyone know what should be a secret is to tell Eddie to keep it to himself. You can bet within half an hour all the world will know!

For the record Penrith won the Grand Final in fine style 19-12 and I was pleased to go into the Panthers dressing room and congratulate them on such a fine win. It was a wonderful match for skipper Royce Simmons who would later in his career come to England to coach Hull FC.

Simmons had played a blinder, scoring two tries for the first time in his career, and seeing it was his last game before retiring it was a fitting end to a great career. A true legend in the history of the Panthers and what a time to score a brace of four pointers. Sadly he wasn't awarded the Clive Churchill Medal for best player on the field. That went to Bradley Clyde from Canberra who played well but Simmons was the star that day.

After receiving the GF Trophy, Simmons, in his country laid back style, acknowledged the Penrith fans for their support and threatened to have a drink with ALL of them!

Knowing Mr Simmons very well indeed I can bet he tried his best to do what he had threatened.

My old club winning the title, a good time visiting friends and family – even if it was for a short time – made it a near perfect year and Sky had asked me to sign an extension to my contract so things were looking up big time!

15

Stevo: **Clean Sheets**

It wasn't long after the Grand Final trip to Sydney that we were on the plane back to Australia for what we hoped would be a great 1992 Lions tour. It looked good because GB had produced a strong, solid side and we were hopeful they could bring back the Ashes to England for the first time since 1970.

Before that we had the pleasure of broadcasting the Wales v Papua New Guinea match in Swansea and I arrived late that Friday evening at our hotel which was over in the Mumbles.

Eddie asked me to go with him to watch the Kumuls train as we had no idea what they looked like or how to pronounce their names. To be truthful I was done in by the travelling and just wanted to relax. So I convinced Eddie to go on his own whilst I settled into the hotel bar and nursed a gin and tonic. I could tell Eddie wasn't too impressed but I didn't feel a hundred per cent and told him so in no uncertain terms.

"Mate, you go and just let me know any tricky names to deal with!"

I wouldn't say he stormed out but there was a touch of tension in the air and I'm sure I could see his big nose sniff and point upwards – always a sign Eddie's none too pleased.

Many hours later he stormed back into the hotel with

that big hooter of his looking somewhat redder than usual and swearing under his breath. It soon transpired the PNG squad had turned out for training all dressed the same in beanie hats, scarves and tracksuits, and for Eddie it was a complete waste of time.

"Any difficult names then to look out for?" I asked.

I'm not quite sure what he said whilst disappearing into the lift but I surmised it was rude.

He calmed down later after I bought him a drink and we laughed out loud at the waste of time he had endured.

It also reminded us of an incident that happened at Hull KR's ground when we drove over the Pennines on a cold wet night to see the Rovers' players trot out for training looking all the same.

Later on we would see much the same when Brisbane came over to play Wigan in the World Club Challenge to see who the World's best was. That was the night the Broncos entered the packed out Central Park Stadium all with shaved heads to boos from the Wigan fans! A nightmare to call.

We all wondered if the Kumuls could handle the pace and strength of this effective Wales outfit which included a swathe of former Union stars who had crossed the divide. Jonathan Davies, John Devereux and Jonathan Griffiths were top names from the 15-a-side code and we expected a big crowd. We were not disappointed as it was a full house.

During the game some drunk idiot climbed the steep ladder and joined us on the gantry. How on earth he did it is beyond belief. He was well and truly drunk and even requested me to give him a light for his cigarette. I don't know why but I replied: "Sorry mate, I don't smoke!"

Eddie quickly realised there could be trouble so pressed the studio key to ask for security.

"Security," was the reply, "... we don't have any," was added.

I told him to go back down but he looked out towards the opposite stand and said, "You get a good view up here," before amazingly wobbling down the ladder to the fans in the stand underneath us.

It was the first time such a thing had happened and from then on we had security at every game.

The match itself went a bit one-sided but the Welsh fans lapped it up and created a fantastic atmosphere. And somehow both of us got through naming the Kumuls without too much embarrassment because when you read the team sheet it looked like someone had thrown a box of scrabble tiles on to a sheet of paper.

That morning I had received a phone call from four mates of mine from Australia who were in the UK for a holiday. They wanted to go to the game but it was a sell out and they couldn't get tickets, so they asked me if I could help, seeing as they had travelled over on the train from London.

I managed to get them some press and camera passes and handed them over in the pub across from the ground two hours before kick off. I told them that once they were inside the ground to mingle with fans in the open stand.

It was whilst the national anthems were being played that I noticed a steward showing them the position at the side of the pitch for the press photographers. The buggers had shown their passes and were now being taken to pitch-side. They soon realised I was perched up high on the TV gantry and started waving their arms at me in a way that only drunk people can.

I ignored them and hoped they would just disappear.

PNG proved no match for Wales and we looked forward to the after match reception for a bite to eat and the odd drink with the players. It turned out to be quite a night when, midway through the speeches, the wife of one of the players ran down the middle of the hall, did two cartwheels and a double somersault, finishing up in front of the stage – supported by yahoos and whoops throughout! It was spectacular to say the least and added to a bizarre function where later in the evening the Kumuls started to sing.

It may be a surprise to you that these boys can sing in harmony like no other group on earth. It's a joy to listen to and I never tire of hearing their charming renditions of their local songs which I always request when I get the chance. They are such nice people and it's difficult to believe that some of the tribes on the islands practiced cannibalism not so long ago!

I had the pleasure of being involved in PNG's first ever tour to Europe in 1987 where they played Great Britain and France. I was asked by their coach to help them out with the scrums for the France game that was played in Carcassonne.

It was an interesting ten days in France where the coach handed out sheets of paper on the morning of the game, which I thought were tactics. It turned out it was a song sheet with the national anthem of PNG written on it. Great singers yes, but so many players came from different Islands with different languages that many of them didn't realise they had a national anthem! It didn't take them long to get it all together and it was amazing to listen to.

Sadly, while they lined up for the anthem to be played over the loudspeakers only the first few bars of the music came blaring out. Then, before they had sung a note, the tape stopped.

What didn't stop was our energy to keep the flag flying in rugby league terms and we were delighted when we got the nod for the 1992 Lions Ashes tour down under. This time there were no business class seats and no five star hotels. But it didn't matter, we were back on tour and who cared if we had to rough it in economy hotels. The fact was we were going!

The budget was tight but it helped that I was going back to Sydney anyway so that was one fare saved. However, poor Ian Proctor was only allowed to go if he paid for his own hotels, food and travel in Australia. He did get a free return flight to Sydney but that was it, the rest was up to him.

It proved not to be a problem seeing I suggested he bunk in with me at the hotels which were being paid for by Sky. All we did was book a twin room, so that solved the sleeping arrangements until our first night in Canberra where our first broadcast was coming from. The hotel was happy to sort out a twin room … that is if they had one, which they didn't! Fortunately there was a large couch in the bedroom which Ian gleefully accepted and after that we twinned for the entire tour.

Ian also suggested we took a trip into the bush to Parkes, a country flavour outback town where the people are mad on rugby league. So much so, tickets for the GB touring game against NSW Country had sold out weeks earlier – and so were all the hotels in Parkes, not a bed to be had for miles anywhere surrounding the town!

We all decided it would be stupid to drive so far into the bush without accommodation, but I found a friend who knew the owner of a rough pub out in the sticks that he had taken over only two weeks earlier.

I quickly rang the pub and asked if there was any room at the Inn.

"Yes there are rooms but not many walls remaining. It's a mess and will take months before it's fit for living in."

"Don't worry about that," I said. "Can you give us clean sheets at least?"

"Yes no problem, but I warn you it's rough and the toilet's at least 25 yards down the corridor."

I put it to the guys and we thought it worth the risk.

Eddie wasn't too sure but we drove the 224 miles knowing at least we had a roof over our heads and we were greeted warmly by the new landlord who insisted he buy us a drink to ease the pain of the near five hour drive.

Mr Hemmings will outline his story but I feel it may be a touch different to mine.

The new landlord produced sandwiches and a good atmosphere was building, but so was Eddie's fear of what the rooms were going to be like. And when he looked at the room he refused to stay there, point blank!

Yes it wasn't the Ritz, and I've slept in rat-infested places around the globe that even cockroaches wouldn't entertain. But this was worse, although it had a roof and a toilet even if it took seven minutes to get there!

We had a bust-up and we headed into the other bar to 'discuss' the problem. I went ape shit, called him a snob and asked how he could insult the new pub owner by refusing to sleep upstairs after his hospitality had been accepted by us all.

It's probably the only time we have both had an all-out slanging match. Yes many tiffs but nothing compared to this. It was full-on.

Eddie threatened to take the car and find a hotel despite the knowledge that all accommodation was full for miles around. He then decided to sleep in the car until he realised it was freezing outside.

Things finally calmed down and after several beers we all couldn't care less where we slept.

We got up the following morning, had a solid breakfast and drove back to Sydney with the knowledge Great Britain had won and what a great bloke the new landlord was ... we even had clean pillows.

Argument? What argument. Such is life working with a snob.

16

Eddie: Five Star Accommodation?

The 1992 British Lions left these shores for the tour of Australia with high hopes of bringing home the Ashes for the first time since 1970.

The preparation for the tour had been good from a playing point of view. In 1991 the Welsh had been born again after an absence of seven years, and the likes of Jonathan Davies, John Devereux, Jonathan Griffiths, David Young, Paul Moriarty and company had all by now crossed the great divide and joined the paid ranks. All were knocking on the door for a place on that 1992 Australasian tour. The Kumuls of Papua New Guinea had provided the first international opposition for the Welsh at the Vetch Field in Swansea on October 27th that year.

The occasion was marked by a 13 try 68-nil demolition of the Papua New Guineans. It was the highest ever score recorded in Welsh rugby league history, and inevitably their inspirational skipper Davies had stolen all the headlines with a personal haul of 24 points from two tries and eight goals. I remember proclaiming on the night that the Vetch Field had risen to him for such a fantastic display.

Two stories of that Test stand out. First the previous day we had travelled to Swansea early with the intention of watching the Kumuls in training. Now South Wales in October is hardly the South Pacific is it? We found out where they were training and for purely identification purposes we headed off to watch them in their final run before the match. Imagine my horror when I saw them emerge from the dressing room on a gloomy and grey afternoon, all dressed in black track suits, black gloves and black beany hats. Added to which most of them had moustaches and basically they were all looking like peas in a pod! I had to try though and as they were put through their paces on that captains run, there I was in the middle of them – with a team sheet, pen and notebook in hand – shadowing each and every one of them. I was desperate for some clue as to whether it was Korul Sinemau, Tuksy Karu or captain Stanley Haru I was looking at! It was, needless to say, a fruitless exercise!

Thankfully with a 68-nil scoreline against them, it didn't really matter the following evening when over 11,500 Welsh folk turned up to see their former Union heroes in this totally different and foreign game. They did really well though and I remember the game as much for the skill that was on show as for a bizarre incident that occurred high up in the roof of the stand on the TV gantry that night.

Stevo and I were waxing lyrical and enjoying what we were witnessing from some of the greats of the Welsh game. It was midway through the second half when Stevo got a tap on the shoulder from a somewhat inebriated supporter who asked him whether he had a match with which to light his cigarette! The gantry was accessed by a ladder that was pinned to one of the pillars holding up the roof. It was a 60 foot vertical climb. Difficult enough when you are stone cold sober, almost impossible I imagine if you've got more than a few beers on board. Anyway this character had somehow made it up to the gantry and said: "Eh Stevo, it's a bloody good view up here isn't it? You haven't got a light have you?"

Stevo was completely unfazed. I heard him say: "Sorry pal I don't smoke!" when suddenly he realised this wasn't a member of our camera crew or our production team but a supporter who somehow had climbed the ladder on to the gantry alongside us! There were a few moments of silence – or dead air as we call it – as we ushered the guy off the gantry and back down the ladder! How the bloke survived the climb up and down I'll never know, but he did and there was a steward waiting for him at the bottom of the ladder to help him on his way out of the ground. I often wonder if he ever did get a light for that cigarette!

Anyway the Welsh had well and truly announced their re-arrival on the International scene and when the squad for the 1992 tour was announced both Devereux and Davies were among the 32 named that April. Injuries obviously played a part in the final make-up of the squad and, as luck would have it, Jonathan Davies had to withdraw with a pelvic bone injury and so couldn't make the trip as a player. He did go though as an interested spectator – and also renewed some old acquaintances after a successful off season with the Canterbury Bankstown club in the ARL.

As luck would have it we were going over to cover the tour as well. Great Britain's loss was our gain and I pushed hard for Jonathan to be involved in our commentary team. He was, after all, one of the biggest names in the game at that time, and his presence with us would add a little extra clout, I thought, to our presentations. The contract was duly signed so he would be on duty with us for our first game of that tour in Canberra against the Raiders.

*****

The Lions had been away from home since the middle of May and had played three games in Papua New Guinea. In the first they beat the Highland Zone in Goroka, then lost to the Island Zone three days later, followed by victory over the Kumuls in a fully-fledged international on May 31st in Port Moresby. On their way to Canberra they had beaten a Queensland Residents XIII 14-10.

We eventually caught up with them in Canberra on a really chilly night on June 5th, just 24 hours before our first match broadcast back home. The flight from the UK to Australia is long – over 24 hours of course. Stevo was already back in Sydney and the arrangement was the crew and myself would meet him in the airport en-route to Canberra on the way to the Raiders' home in the Australian capital. However, the best laid plans don't always go smoothly and as we arrived in Sydney the news filtered through there was thick fog in Canberra and flights were being heavily delayed. So we sat and waited for our flight while the pea souper cleared.

We eventually got to Canberra in the middle of the afternoon, a good three or four hours late. And by that stage, with the travelling and jet-lag, all I wanted to do was go to bed and sleep for a couple of years! But we still had to head down to the Raiders Stadium to see the captains run, and more important, get the names of the 17 men that would be taking the field against Great Britain the following night. So off we went.

To be fair Tim Sheens, the coach of the Raiders at the time, couldn't have been more helpful. He let us watch the entire session and then came to us afterwards and named his side. Men like New Zealand international Sean Hoppe would be on the wing and the great Ricky Stuart, Test half back for the Aussies, would be leading the attack from scrum half. Great Britain would have it all on to get the serious part of their tour off to a winning start.

The plan was Jonathan would be our sideline eye, Stevo and me in the commentary box, and Nev the producer in touch with London. Some people thought that having Jonathan there was a luxury that wasn't really required. I firmly believed that he would add presence and gravitas to our coverage – he was after all one of the biggest names in the game. I fought for his involvement. I was convinced it would work.

The game kicked off and Great Britain started well. Canberra were due to play a Winfield Cup game the following day but had taken the match on and it was to be the Lions' final major game in preparation for the First Test that was to be played six days later. The starting line-up of the Raiders looked really strong on paper with Brett Mullins, Ricky Stuart captaining them and Sean Hoppe on one wing. But that didn't last long. Ricky Stuart for instance played in the number seven jersey for about ten minutes before he was replaced by another number seven. Nobody was being fooled because the latest number seven was from an indigenous background!

Great Britain led 20-6 at half time. The tourists were playing well but by this time I wasn't that concerned with the performance or the scoreline. The Raiders' try had been scored by number five, Sean Hoppe. I had been waxing lyrical about him: "A Kiwi international, we will see Hoppe again on the last leg of this tour when Britain play New Zealand. "What a try by Hoppe – a real danger to Great Britain later in the tour." It was all Hoppe, Hoppe, Hoppe. The conversion was taken and scored and Nev – who was producing in the commentary box – indicated I should hand down to the sideline for a comment on the Hoppe try by Jonathan immediately after the kick. So with words something like: "A great try then from Canberra's Sean

Hoppe improved by Ricky Stuart with the boot, let's join Jonathan at pitchside. Jonathan this guy Hoppe is quite a player isn't he?"

There followed a pregnant pause from our sideline eye. He then uttered the words: "That's not Sean Hoppe, its Michael Spinks and I don't mean the boxer by the same name. This is Michael Spinks of Canberra Raiders who's scored the try in the corner. Hoppe has been replaced!"

I was stunned. You never ever point up a colleague's mistake. It's just not professional in our game. What I didn't know was that number five Sean Hoppe had been replaced by ... number five Michael Spinks! I looked down at the team sheet, Spinks wasn't even mentioned anywhere! I scribbled a note to Nev, "Get Down there and tell him not to ever do that again," and within seconds back came a note in the opposite direction, "You tell him. You picked him!" To say I was flustered was the understatement of the year. All that determination 24 hours earlier after a flight half way round the world to actually get things right and do a professional job had fallen in an almighty heap!

As soon as the game was over I threw down the microphone and headed to the sideline to confront Jonathan. I was raging. "Don't you ever do that to me again!" I hollered. And to be fair Jonathan was full of apologies. He knew he'd made a bit of a ricket.

It turned out to be a shambles of a match all round. The Lions won 24-12, good on paper. But after the game Maurice Lindsay, the tour manager, accused the Canberra club of insulting international rugby league by fielding a virtual reserve side and sending on a total of seven substitutes – three more than the permitted quota. What a shame they'd taken it upon themselves to do this and then added insult to injury by not telling anyone of the number switches which made me look – not for the first time and not for the last – a bit of a goose! Still you learn by experiences like that.

Six days later the Lions lost the first Test in Sydney by 22-6, so it was off to Melbourne for the second with matches in between against NSW Country out in Parkes, Parramatta and finally Newcastle Knights. We were covering the games against Parramatta and Newcastle live for the viewers back home. The Country game wasn't on our broadcast schedule but we thought we'd better go and keep tabs on things just the same.

*****

It's quite a car journey from Sydney to Parkes but we set off knowing it would take us at least two days. A hotel was needed for the night, before we got back to Sydney the following day. Stevo had elected himself the courier and was the man charged with the task of sorting out our accommodation. As such he insisted we had to stay in Parkes itself. Basically Parkes is a small town out in the middle of Australian nowhere but apparently with a great social scene that we would all enjoy after the game had finished.

The 'hotel' that had been booked for us turned out to be owned by a long lost pal of Stevo's and basically was a 12 by 12 room above a pub with four makeshift beds erected where Stevo, me, Nev and Ian Proctor would be able to lay our heads for the night. The cost? Ten dollars per head payable in advance via Stevo! The room? Well it left a lot to be desired. Holes in the walls where it looked like someone had punched their fists through. I'm sure I heard something scurrying about underneath the beds too. And the en-suite? That was a room at the end of a dark corridor with cold water in a cracked, filthy and stained sink and the toilet for all four of us to use was one that just about flushed when you pulled the chain.

Five star accommodation? Hardly! Quite simply not what I was used to anyway. Now I don't often moan all that much (ok I am known here and there as Victor Meldrew) but I did have a go about the hotel that Stevo had fixed up for us and I was quite keen to move out and find another billet for the night. But Stevo had paid the money over, it was his mate, it was only for one night – you get the picture. He was a little reluctant to move!

We adjourned to the bar and downed a few and the guy who ran the place seemed a decent enough bloke. We got on pretty well, so much so that I suggested that we should all have a bite to eat together and then he could join us at the match. That was the moment the balloon went up. I was accused of being a snob, of having moaned all day about the state of the room, the state of the place, even the quality of the bed sheets (they were sleeping bags from memory) and now I was asking mine host out for a meal and offering to take him to the match. To put it mildly, Stevo was far from impressed and he let his feelings be known.

There was quite a bit of finger pointing and threats of this and that. The atmosphere wasn't the best and it lasted for a couple of hours. I can honestly say it was the first and just about the only time that Stevo and I fell out, but after several more beers and a British victory by 24-6 we buried the hatchet and somewhat drunkenly made our way back to the digs for the night.

This time I didn't hear the snoring and moaning from the bed next to me. I think I was far too inebriated for that. But Ian wasn't so lucky and on the way home the following day he regaled us with stories of the noise that emanated from the 'Creature of the Black Lagoon' that night.

I thought: "I've been there, done that and got the T shirt!" I made a mental note and sent a memo to myself that day:

never share a bedroom with Stevo ever again. From that day to this I never have and never will!

But the tour progressed. We lost the first Test in Sydney – nothing new there of course – and we headed off to the second Test in Melbourne more in hope than in anticipation. Before we'd left these shores, the Sky promotions team had filmed a trailer for what was to come with some of the biggest names in the game. The likes of Garry Schofield and Andy Gregory had been filmed waving a Union Jack behind a little drummer boy with smoke billowing all around. The British were coming all right was the message we wanted to get across and we had the players to reclaim the RL Ashes after a lapse of fully 20 years.

We entered Princes Park, Melbourne, on the back of a 22-6 beating in Sydney. On our way to Victoria, deep in the heart of Aussie Rules territory and way before the Melbourne Storm had re-written the history books in that part of the world, we had beaten the NSW Country boys in Parkes, lost in Parramatta 16-22 but then beaten Newcastle Knights 22-nil. Hopes were high that we could turn the tide around.

The party had suffered a blow though with the loss of inspirational skipper Ellery Hanley who was injured and on his way home. Garry Schofield was the man to celebrate his official appointment as tour captain and lead the British to a record-equalling 23 point win in the first ever GB-Aussie Test to be played in the city.

Wigan had provided the entire pack and the tactic proved a masterstroke. No one single club had ever before provided all six forwards at this level – and two others in the backs with Martin Offiah and Shaun Edwards. There were a total of eight Wigan players on duty that unforgettable night when Great Britain claimed their best win on Australian soil since 1958.

It was a real joy to commentate on. Stevo was on great

form, as we all were. He was relishing the fact that at last when he got back home to Sydney he would have something to boast about. The night was summed up completely when Graham Steadman, the Castleford full back who'd played brilliantly in defence all game, linked up with the attack with just seven minutes to go to scorch over in the corner for the Lions' penultimate try. Now there was a hint of a forward pass in the build-up but Stevo in summarising the try simply said: "Maybe a hint of a forward pass from Offiah to Steadman but who cares. Britain have restored a 19 point advantage and surely now cannot be beaten so they have won this Test match."

Another Welshman, Kevin Ellis of Warrington, was providing comments from the sideline for us on the night. Kevin was in the squad but not picked for the match. As Steadman and the rest of the British boys celebrated the try I handed down to Kev. "What's the mood down there Kev?" I remember asking. "Oh Eddie the boys are buzzin'," came the reply. And ever since – still to this day – whenever Kevin and I meet up at the odd match he always comes over, shakes my hand warmly and yells: "The boys are buzzin' Eddie!"

Another of my great memories happened afterwards, back at our hotel which we were sharing with the team in all the excitement of the win. It was Ian's birthday and Garry Schofield, the victorious Lions skipper and great pal of ours at the time, joined us with a birthday cake full of candles singing Happy Birthday to Ian to kick start a night of great celebrations. Great stuff, great memories and the greatest ever Test win that I have ever called.

I also remember that in the commentary box next to us at the stadium and calling the game for the New Zealand audience back home was the Kiwi scrum half Gary Freeman. His joy at seeing the Aussies put to the sword rivalled ours and he was smiling just as widely as all of us that night, loving every moment of describing the Australian demise to his folks back home!

Sadly our euphoria wasn't to last long. Seven days later we were at Lang Park in Brisbane for the deciding third Test and Mal Meninga stepped up to the plate on his record 37th Test appearance for Australia, kicking four goals and claiming the match winning try in a 16-10 Aussie win. That was a massive anti-climax after all the hype and a disappointing encounter which failed to live up to the pre-match billing. Once again the Aussies showed they are the masters of physical and mental strength at just the right time. Seven days after a whipping in Melbourne they rose to claim yet another series win against Great Britain. The wait for the Ashes to come home was to go on … and on!

17

Eddie: Costa Cost

Sadly that was to be our last trip down under for quite a while. Seismic changes lay ahead for the game worldwide. Little did we know that things would never be the same again.

The winter game produced its usual fair share of thrills and excitement. Wigan were ruling the roost as they had done for much of the previous decade. But when they went out to Brisbane in 1994 to face the Broncos for one of the few World Club Challenge games ever to be played on Aussie soil, rumours were afoot that big changes were on the way for rugby league.

It was June 1st, 1994, to be precise. Wigan had won the League and Cup double and had topped the season off with a Premiership Final win at Old Trafford against Castleford. It was the close season of course but Wigan had accepted the challenge from the Broncos to travel 10,000 miles to take them on in their own back yard in the hope of proving they were the best club side on the planet.

Over 54,000 people had squeezed their way into the ANZ stadium to watch the game unfold. Not for the first time the Australians had written off Wigan's chances. They were after all coming over at the back end of a tiring domestic season. Brisbane were right in the middle of the Winfield Cup campaign and Wigan could be excused for believing this was a well-deserved end of season holiday with the game thrown in to help pay for the festivities. From what I'm told there was a bit of partying to be enjoyed, but the Wigan players had a meeting at which they said they were going to give the game their best shot.

And give it their best shot they did – in spades. Jason Robinson, Barrie-Jon Mather and Denis Betts scored the tries and Frano Botica kicked four goals. For the first time ever on Aussie soil, Wigan ruled the world, winning a great game by 20-14. My Sky colleague Phil Clarke played in that game and says it was one of his greatest ever victories. It was a match that was a dream to play in with so much to savour and gain from the victory.

So the story goes, officials of Rupert Murdoch's News International organisation were inside the stadium watching the game as well and were so impressed with what they saw that apparently it was there that the first thoughts of a global game under one banner – a Super League – were mooted. The ball was rolling towards what turned out to be a bitter and turbulent time as Rupert Murdoch and his great rival Kerry Packer started jousting for overall control of the game.

There was then a visit to the UK by some of the top officials of News International. The big questions were about the state of the game in England and how did we, as observers, broadcasters and journalists, believe a major switch in emphasis from winter to summer would be received by the people who mattered – those running the game, and perhaps more importantly, the men running the clubs.

It should be remembered at this stage in proceedings, that clubs were being paid something like £30,000 if their games were televised. And it was only the club staging the match at their own ground that would benefit. Hence when

I was asked for my opinion, I never envisaged that a big multi-million pound deal was in the offing and I indicated that I believed it would be unlikely that clubs like Wigan, St Helens and Leeds would give up the opportunity of cashing in on bumper Boxing Day and New Year's Day crowds just to switch to summer football. Wembley, the Premiership Final and international rugby league would also surely be affected. I thought it was, while a very good idea, highly unlikely to be accepted at the highest levels.

How wrong could I have been? Of course I wasn't privy to the top level negotiations that obviously were taking place. I thought, wrongly, that interest would peter out and come September the rugby league season would pick up where it left off. It would mean long summer months of inactivity and my thoughts turned of how best to spend them.

My children were all still at school back then and my wife Carole and I were looking forward to the usual round of summer holidays with them. How could we extend that? Well obviously the answer was – if we could afford it, and we just about could – to buy a little place abroad, preferably just a couple of hours flight away so that we could spend long summer holidays in the sunshine getting ready for the following season.

It was late spring of 1995 and we had headed off to Spain to look for a property. It wouldn't be anything flash, just a one bedroomed apartment but big enough to take a sofa bed in the lounge room and maybe three singles in the bedroom so that we could all go away every year and enjoy the summer together. We headed off to Alicante one weekend, found the perfect place right on a golf course (I was pretty keen back then) and we decided that perhaps this was the place.

It was overlooking the driving range on a golf complex called Villamartin on the outskirts of a town called Torrevieja on the Costa Blanca. Perfect! But while we'd been there on our shopping trip, the weather hadn't really been all that kind. We were due home on the Monday evening and while we had dinner on the Sunday night we took the decision that if the sun was shining the following morning it was obviously meant to be and we would complete the sale. If it was dull, or worse still raining, we would walk away.

We awoke on the Monday and of course the sun was cracking the flags. We saw the agent, the local notary, wrote the cheque for the deposit, chose the furniture and then legged it to Alicante Airport for the flight home. We were suddenly property owners in a foreign land. Happy Days!

I'll never forget the following week. Suddenly all the talk was of a switch to summer rugby. Easter was on the horizon. The clubs were in their regular monthly meeting and apparently, so the story goes, Maurice Lindsay left to take an important phone call. He returned a few minutes later to announce to the chairmen that he had just had a phone conversation with Rupert Murdoch in Australia, who had offered a deal to move the game to summer in exchange for a contract worth £85 million!

It was a no-brainer. Virtually all the clubs were in financial strife. Here before them was an offer of money that would wipe out all the debt with a few million each besides. It didn't take long to take the vote and summer rugby league was on the way. Just a few provisos though – Paris and London had to be included in what would be called the European Super League and clubs would have to merge – still to this day a dirty word! Widnes and Warrington would merge to become Cheshire. Rochdale, Salford, Swinton and Oldham would become Manchester. Hull and Hull KR would merge into Humberside. Castleford, Wakefield and Featherstone would become Calder. But Wigan, Leeds, Bradford, St Helens and a few others would remain as they were. Despite all the obvious repercussions, all the hands flew up to vote in favour in the meeting and summer rugby league was going to start in April, 1996. My holiday dreams were up in smoke and it would cost me a couple of thousand quid into the bargain. A deposit is a deposit and it wasn't coming back very easily from Spain!

Inevitably there were problems brewing at the clubs. Widnes and Warrington to merge? Hull and Hull KR to join across the river? No chance. So the clubs threw out the proposals at grass roots level and back they went for another meeting hastily called for the following weekend. This time the money went up another £2 million and the mergers weren't a vital component anymore, but London and Paris still were. So how the game would get down to ten clubs plus the two big cities was up to the power brokers again. The deal was voted through and this time there was to be no turning back.

I'll never forget the day. It was the Saturday of the Grand National at Aintree and a massive press conference had been called at Wigan that morning. I was there for Sky along with Neville Smith, the big boss Vic Wakeling and lawyers from both sides – the whole box and dice. The cameras were rolling, the press seats packed and at the allotted hour the biggest ever announcement was made in the history of British Rugby League. Obviously delighted that the future of both the game and the Sky commitment to it was secure, my all-consuming feeling was one of: "Bloody hell, what about my £2,000 sitting in a bank account in Spain?"

We did the interviews, said all the right things and then I thought I've got to tell someone about this. So I pulled Nev to one side and confided that I'd just bought the flat in Spain and this news was going to cost me a fortune! His reaction? He creased over, doubled up in laughter and told Vic and the rest of my colleagues what I'd just told him. To say I didn't get much sympathy is the understatement of the century.

I had a decision to make – pull out of the deal or go ahead with it and see how it would go. I chose the latter and have no regrets whatsoever. Our family have met some fabulous people out in Spain and we had a number of wonderful times playing golf and enjoying the lifestyle (Carole is a fluent Spanish speaker so that really helped) and we don't regret taking the plunge at all. The only problem was that EasyJet and Ryannair weren't flying at the time, so to nip across for a short period stay was a bit costly to say the least.

But we stuck it out for a few years before eventually selling up around about the time the Peseta was lost to the Euro. Overall it cost us a good few bob but it was worth it for the experience, and of course it gave the lads on the crew, and still does to this day, the story to tell of Eddie the bloke who always times his big decisions in life to perfection. Yeah right!

18

Stevo: Cardboard Hankie

It was in 1994 that I was becoming a bit cheesed off at flying back to England, working the season and then flying back to Sydney to yet another winter period.

Most people think Sydney is sunshine forever. Far from it and it can get pretty cold and miserable in the winter months. Also I was missing the chance to be with the kids in a summer where we could go to the beach, swim in the sea and do what Aussies do when the weather is good – chill out.

It was also the time when champions Wigan made a bold move to actually go and play the World Club Challenge down under against a Brisbane side brimming with superstars. I wanted the English clubs to do well but not many thought a team from the Northern Hemisphere could beat an Aussie club on their own ground.

Some called it fantasy rugby, but Wigan pulled out all the stops that year and did what most thought impossible. To travel to the other side of the World to face an Aussie side on their own turf, most people thought they had no chance. Well Wigan ignored the naysayers and became stars in their own right by beating the odds-on favourites 20-14 on their own ground.

It not only shook up a nation, it made the top brass at a certain organisation think perhaps this could be the start

A photo of the crew from our early days at Sky Sports

The GB v Australia matches have given us some memorable moments. On this occasion at Wembley in 1990 GB gained a 19-12 win

© RLPhotos.com

The 1991 Challenge Cup Final between Wigan and St Helens at the old Wembley Stadium with a youthful looking Ian Proctor

Treading the boards at the City Varieties theatre was a great experience ... once we'd cobbled together a script in the pub next door!

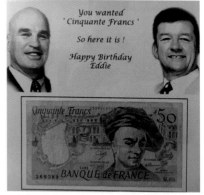

You wanted 'Cinquante Francs'
So here it is !
Happy Birthday Eddie

The 50 Francs I owed Eddie. I don't think he's ever forgiven me for that stunt in the restaurant

Former Leeds and Wakefeld player Garry Spencer looks bemused at our antics on an early *Boots 'n' All*

Seen here in New Zealand in 2010, the Kumuls gave Eddie some identification problems in South Wales but boy can those fellas sing!

"Fancy a bash at that Stevo?" Eddie doing the pre-match introduction for the 2007 Grand Final at Old Trafford

© RLPhotos.com

The consumate professional, Eddie presents the Sky Sports coverage of the 2009 Four Nations with RFL Chief Executive Nigel Wood

© RLPhotos.com

We've had some great fun covering games in France and the Catalans fans certainly add a splash of colour!

© RLPhotos.com

As commentators we are supposed to be impartial but seeing Great Britain win has always been special. Here the team celebrate victory over New Zealand at Knowsley Road in 2006
© RLPhotos.com

Stevo at Headingley hosting the Albert Goldthorpe Medal awards in 2009, won that year by Hull KR's Michael Dobson

Travelling to the UK for the rugby league season gives Stevo the opportunity to catch up with his family. Here he celebrates the 40th anniversary of Dewsbury's Championship victory with his Auntie Doris
© RLPhotos.com

Our co-presenters do a superb job in Sky Sports' coverage of rugby league. Here Bill Arthur prepares pre-match in the mobile home and Terry O'Connor, Barry McDermott and Stuart Cummings are in the midst of calling a game

Silk Cut, the former sponsors of the Challenge Cup, used to push the boat out big time with their parties

The World Club Challenge games present a great spectacle in the early weeks of the season. It's always good to see the Super League teams take the trophy but in 2013 Melbourne Storm were worthy winners

© RLPhotos.com

We would never be able to make the rugby league programmes without the brilliant crew we have at Sky Sports. Here are photos of some of the special people who do such a superb job

Producer June Fairhurst, Director Mark Smith and Martin Carroll the best vision mixer in the World

Sue Goldstone, the makeup lady who works miracles

Ian Proctor, a fount of knowledge on all things rugby league

Rhodri Jones from the RFL with Outside Broadcast Production Manager Kevin Connor

Heidi Cannavo and Brian Middlehurst

Floor Manager Dave Redfearn sparring with Martin Carroll

Richard Thomas, our man in
charge of security

Andy Syres, James Brooks and
Jim Oulton

Pete Fairhurst, Andy Syres, Katie
Millward and Jon Wells

Ray Fry the Manager of
Telegenic Outside Broadcasting
at his retirement

Billy Painter, Steve Owen and Ben Proe

John Heyes, Mr Mobile Home

We mustn't forget our boss and great mate Nev Smith. Here Eddie tells him again he's worth more than a hundred quid!

Rumours of Stevo's retirement have often done the rounds but this time it's for real

We'll always be the best of mates!

of a global revolution. Rumour has it some of the senior executives at Rupert Murdoch's News International were amazed at the pace and ferocity of that game. It was an eye-opener to those who had not realised what a great game rugby league is.

The rumours began to get bigger and some pundits started thinking of league becoming global. I started thinking wow, maybe they could switch to summer in the UK and play at the same time as they do in Australia. It was a no-brainer. Tours could be held without fixtures being compromised, and let's face it, the summer in Blighty hardly cracks the flagstones for more than a few days in the year.

Obviously I was all for it. Summer back-to-back. What a boost that would be for yours truly. At long last the chance to see a summer down under. We didn't hold our breath but on occasions I took the liberty to push for a switch to summer. I wanted to be the Richie Benaud of rugby league, following the sunshine all year round.

It was at Oldham where we were filming a promo for the upcoming weekend game that I looked down the camera and pleaded for RL boss Maurice Lyndsay to think about going to summer. I can still feel the wind and sleet hitting the umbrella so hard it nearly blew me away as I uttered the words: "Come on Maurice. The players and fans need better conditions than this. We have to go for summer."

I'm not silly enough to think that it swayed the decision, but the dangling of the carrot to our British clubs of £85 million from Mr Murdoch certainly did. Most of our clubs in this country were deep in debt – some worse than others – and this was a chance to wipe the slate, and Mr Lyndsay knew it too.

Eddie has gone into great detail about how mergers and new clubs were going to be introduced to create a Super League in which teams from around Europe would compete.

Sadly, the only real bonuses were the introduction of London and Paris, and eventually Catalans from Perpignan when Paris proved a problem. We had of course high hopes of flying into Barcelona, Prague and Munich. Boy my passport was going to have more stamps than the post office!

Not surprisingly I was ecstatic, but given poor old Eddie had just sunk his money into a flat in Spain, he was sporting a grimace that made him look like a battered prune. The fact that Super League would run through the summer meant that the flat would stand empty for most of the hot season, which created a lot of hilarity when it was realised my mate had splashed out good money to own a place in the land of paella.

I know he kept it for a few years but he eventually gave in and sold it at a loss and the flat did create another fall-out between us.

Along with a certain Mr Chris Tate, a former league player who was working in our department at the time, I suggested we find out the address of Eddie's place in Spain and request brochures for stair lifts, walk in baths, surgical appliances, hearing aids, strong glasses and more that would eventually clog up his letter box to bursting point.

Eddie's neighbour had been to a few games when the pointed nose one had invited him, so we decided to ask him to find out for us. Unfortunately when we enquired he didn't know, but thought his wife did, so we rang and asked if she could find out. What we didn't know was she told Eddie straight away, hoping she wouldn't be hassled by those men again!

One phone call and we were rumbled. Eddie went ballistic because for some reason he thought we were trying to chat her up! This time it was Eddie's turn to hit the roof but thankfully after I explained he realised there had been a few crossed wires and he had got the wrong end of the stick. However, he was furious and his words carried far and wide in the empty stadium at Sheffield.

It all blew over and our attention turned to a party that Eddie was having to celebrate his 40th birthday. It was being held on a large barge on the canal near his home in Warrington. He insisted we all come in fancy dress, and not surprisingly Eddie dressed up as a cavalier prince – sword and all, feather in his hat and a wide smile to match. He looked regal to say the least.

I decided to go as a tramp, so set about by buying a lot of old clothes from a charity shop and turning myself into a what I thought was as near to the real thing as possible. Unfortunately I did too good a job and when I tried to get on to the barge the bouncer at the entrance told me to piss off, "We don't want people like you around here".

I didn't think I looked that convincing but it was only when I showed him the invitation that he laughed and let me on board. To be fair I had rolled around in the mud for a while, doused myself with turps and smelled like a sewer. I actually thought about rubbing some dog shit on my hat but I felt that might be stepping over the mark so decided against it!

You should have seen the faces on the other guests who thought, like the bouncer, that I was the real thing. I hugged Eddie (which didn't go down too well with Prince Charming) until he realised it was his old mate.

Eddie proudly informed the guests it was me and handed me a pint of lager which I lifted high to all and sundry, wished him happy birthday and proceeded to pour the entire contents over my head. Not a drop hit my lips, but the next few did and it turned out to be one of the best parties I've ever been to.

*****

I wouldn't say I looked very classy in the tramp outfit and I'm no Pierre Cardin but in fairness I like to think I dress smart, especially when on TV. A good shirt, nice tie and my trademark hankie in the pocket. Obviously I don't expect the viewers to be going into raptures over my colour selection but it makes me feel comfortable whilst wearing it. The trouble is it didn't take Eddie long to realise what slides into the coat pocket is NOT a proper silk hankie!

On one broadcast break he wondered why the hankie never dropped down and always looked snappy, so he pulled the hankie out to reveal it's a piece of cloth stapled on to a square of cardboard – top quality cardboard I might add – and the long-nosed one went into hysterics whilst calling me a cheat.

Being a solid and proud Yorkshireman I pointed out that buying proper silk hankies cost a fortune, in fact I've seen them priced £20 for ONE, so I substitute a proper silk handkerchief for a fake one.

On my travels from Sydney to London, most of the time I stop over in Dubai where the locals sell huge lengths of cloth for the local ladies to turn into those beautiful dresses. Those shops also have books of samples where often one hundred different designs are on show for easy display. So I purchase the sample books that have gone out of date.

I can get up to four hankies from each sample. That works out at 400 pocket hankies each sample book at a cost of a fiver. Unlike the Artful Dodger I can 'stuff' a pocket or two!

Eddie threatens me most weeks that come my last broadcast at the 2016 Grand Final he will expose me to the audience for being a cheat. Once again I beat him to the mark.

Maybe it's time for me to tell you a few tales about my best buddy who is like a brother to me – and those that have brothers know they can be like chalk and cheese.

I'm not sure which one I am but I know Eddie is the tidiest bloke I've ever met. If you sit with him on the outside catering bus and you drop a crumb, he will quickly wipe it up. If he notices your tie isn't straight or there's a bit of fluff on your coat, he'll fix your tie and brush off the fluff.

Staying in hotels on our travels can prove hilarious. I explained about him being a snob over the Parkes hotel saga, but if you walk into his room and wander into his toilet you can bet the shampoo, soap, hair spray, toothpaste and aftershave are all lined up in order, left to right, largest first and then down to the smallest like guards on parade.

Me, I just throw the wash-bag into the corner and keep it there. Not our long-nosed friend, oh no, it has to be perfect and I kid you not.

I remember one hotel in Brisbane where it was a self-catering style room with a kitchen sink, cooker, washer and dryer which is a big help whilst on tour and it was my turn to host the late morning meeting. The night before I had played host to a bunch of my mates from Sydney who flew up for the Ashes Test and had sent out for pizza and booze. So you can imagine what the room looked like the following morning – a bloody mess.

At about 10.30 I heard this knocking on the door and Neville was outside with some of the crew ready to plan the schedule for the day, only to find a rather dishevelled Stevo stinking of booze with bits of food stuck to my stubble.

Nev was quick off the mark saying we should move back to his room after seeing the road-crash in my room, but Eddie said no worries I'll fix it and he did. Whilst the meeting was taking place, he cleared all the pizza boxes, wiped the tables, washed the glasses, plates, you name it. Everything was wiped, washed, dried and put away in its proper place just before the meeting ended half an hour later and Eddie never stopped adding his penny's worth in the process. And to cap it all off he took out the garbage bag and dumped it down the rubbish chute at the end of the corridor. Now that's what you call a mate!

He may be tidy, proper and a snob but he's always quick to invite you to his home and both he and his lovely wife Carole make you most welcome (I never stay – it's the snoring) and the hospitality is top-class. Although the first time I visited the Hemmings household and walked through the door, the dog fussed around me and before I could say hello it cocked its leg and pissed all over my shoes.

Nice dog, nice welcome!

The second occasion the same dog attacked my trousers and ripped the bottom half to shreds, leaving me no option but to throw them away afterwards. Needless to say the dog was shut away after that. Down boy! What made it worse it was tiny, only about ten inches long

A few years later I arrived at their place only to find the radiator in the living room wasn't working. Being a former plumber I came to their rescue and asked Eddie for an adjustable spanner.

Eddie couldn't find one so got in the car and drove to his local B&Q about three miles away. On his return I grabbed the brand spanking new tool and whacked it against the nut joint and to Eddie's amazement the radiator started to warm up.

"There you go," I said. "All working fine."

"Bloody hell. If I knew you were going to just hit it I could have given you a hammer and not wasted my money!"

He still has the spanner to this day as a testimony, I'm sure, to my plumbing skills.

In the early days when we were getting to know each other I asked him where he was born.

"Oh, Aigburth Heights, Liverpool," came the reply.

I never really took much notice but sometime later I was

driving towards Liverpool Airport and was surprised to see a sign for Eddie's home suburb, so I pulled into a petrol station and enquired where Aigburth Heights was.

"No Heights around here mate, it's as flat as a pancake!"

Later that week and not surprisingly Eddie admitted it sounded a bit posher.

See I told you he was a snob.

Snob or not we had a few laughs that poor old Eddie was unable to make the most of the flat he had bought in Spain through the switch to summer rugby league. It was in a great area with half-a-dozen golf courses. Eddie's a mad keen golfer but not a good one from my experience of playing with him!

Amazingly the area turned out to be where my son Craig was working as an estate agent in Spain, and surprisingly I bumped into my old mate in the same complex where he had the holiday home. He was with a group of golfers that came over each year and they made me welcome to say the least. It was a classy joint and I soon realised what a shame it was for him having to sell it off because the complex had numerous restaurants and bars, a gym, sauna and swimming pool – a paradise away from the cold north of England.

It also came about that later that night I didn't feel too hot. Even though I had kept up with the boys at drinking and eating I was somewhat concerned as this just wasn't a hangover, it was something a touch worse.

The last couple of nights with my son I kept off the drink (you can tell I was ill) and flew back to England a bit worried.

A few years earlier I had passed out before doing a game at Watersheddings, Oldham, and struggled even to get up the ladder to the gantry above. I kept it secret and somehow managed to call the game, but in the end I had to admit to Eddie I was off to see a doctor in Manchester to check out why I was in so much pain in my chest. Obviously I thought it was my heart. It wasn't but that problem came later in Australia.

The Saturday morning I went to have some liquid inserted in … well, shall we say where the sun don't shine, and a radiologist took X-rays.

I was in agony and stripped off, put on a gown and was requested to lie on my side until the doctor came and inserted the tubes up and, well, inside you know where.

Embarrassed? No kidding, course I was and then on seeing the image that came in front of my eyes I started to go bright red in the face. The radiologist turned out to be a beautiful young lady. Oh my God! She disappeared behind the protective curtain to take the X-rays, only to stop halfway and tell me that the tubes had slipped out of my bottom and she would have to tape them in!

Ten minutes later the job was done. Fifteen minutes after that I was rushed to a private hospital in Salford where my gall bladder had to be urgently removed.

Most gall bladder stones can be dissolved or removed by micro surgery but not this 'big' problem. Normally your gall bladder is no bigger than a golf ball. The X-rays showed mine to be as big as a grapefruit.

Five hours in surgery fixed it after they slowly separated it from all my other organs. Evidently I was lucky because if I'd left it another few months I would have been six foot under and pushing up daisies!

The people at the BUPA hospital in Salford were outstanding and I thank them to this day for the care and attention they gave me. And to cap it all, even Eddie came to see me!

But I digress, back to my problem in Spain where I was concerned because I was short of breath. I wondered if it was an asthma attack, but a day later it settled down and

I didn't think anything more about it. Then a week later I flew back to Sydney.

Australia was plagued by bush fires that summer. The Northern Beaches where I lived didn't miss out and we were all scared that we would be evacuated. The sky was a misty red from the fires and I started to struggle with my breathing again. I put it down to all the smoke and ash floating about but my wife Maureen forced me to go see the doctor. After checking me over, the doc realised I was suffering atrial fibrillation, a condition that causes your heart to have an abnormally fast rate.

I lived with this awful problem for a few years never knowing when it would hit me. The medication was a nightmare that made it difficult to sleep or even concentrate. A couple of times I had an attack on air and Eddie would quickly alert Neville to ensure the camera wasn't pointing at me while he took control. In the meantime, I would try to calm down and hope my heart wouldn't create a blood clot.

To give you some idea, a normal heartbeat is like dancing a nice steady waltz, but when atrial fibrillation kicks in, it's like dancing to a combination of rock and roll and punk rock, sending your heart valves crazy and causing a huge risk of a blood clot.

Sometimes it would take many hours for my heart to get back into a normal rhythm but thankfully, after four or five years of uncertainty, I was recommended to Doctor Schilling, a consultant cardiologist at London Bridge Hospital who had been experimenting on a new procedure to help stop such attacks.

Evidently his study had been on pig hearts which are very similar to a human heart. After consultation he said that nobody had accepted his offer to be 'his first human experiment'.

Within one minute I had signed away the papers

exonerating any blame on the medical staff and he operated on me the following morning with great success – and it's been fine ever since. The staff at the hospital were wonderful and that was one 'Schilling' I was glad to pay!

Throughout this time my mate Eddie was resourcefully carrying on without me and again at other times when I had the odd health problem. However, more recently he had his own worries to deal with and that's why nowadays we wear the badges for prostate cancer on TV.

I was stunned when he told me at Castleford two years ago. I couldn't believe it and I cried openly because nobody wants hear that word cancer. Fortunately it seems the medical people diagnosed it in time and hopefully the cancer has now been dealt with. But prostate cancer is the most common cancer in men and, like Eddie says, please get checked out. I certainly did and thankfully I'm OK but I repeat the check regularly each year.

So as you can gather, there have been occasions when it hasn't all been fun and games throughout those 28 years since we met in the foyer at BBC Manchester.

19

Eddie: Five Martin Offiah's

After a shortened winter season in 1995 that ran from August to January 1996 – see the clubs really did love their Boxing Day fixtures – the Super League was born.

The new era, probably the most momentous season since the 22 originals broke away in 1895 to form the Northern Union, got under way on a memorable Friday night in Paris on March 29th, 1996, when Paris St Germain entertained the Sheffield Eagles. Yes, nicknames became part of the scene as well with Wigan Warriors, Bradford Bulls, Leeds Rhinos and London Broncos all becoming recognised parts of the rugby league vocabulary!

The European Super League kicked off in one of the world's greatest cities in front of a crowd of almost 18,000, the largest crowd for an opening day fixture in rugby league for 25 years. It was one of the greatest nights of my broadcasting career. Here we were again at the birth of something special. The Satellite TV revolution had been one thing but here now, six years later, was another. A rebirth of one of the bedrock sports in England. This really was something unique.

The final winter season finished on January 21st. Two rounds of the Challenge Cup had been played, one in January, one in February. We at Sky had been planning for the big kick off to the European Super League for a good eight months.

The word from the bosses at Osterley was that it had to be something special. The question fired back asked whether they really were unhappy with the ground-breaking coverage Sky had given the game that had been so well received since we launched in 1990. The answer to that was no, they loved it. But this was something different now. We had to get the Super League noticed. How were we going to improve something that was already recognised as – well if I'm honest – pretty damned good?

The one major development that was voted through of course was the introduction of the video referee system. If the man in the middle had any doubts about the validity of the try being scored, he would make a signal of a box and ask the video referee to check it out. It was the brainchild of Neville Smith and Greg McCallum, the former referee from Australia (he just happened to be the man in the middle in Brisbane for the Wigan game in 1994 by the way) who by now had hung up his whistle and was the referees' controller in the Super League.

Between them Nev and Greg devised a scheme that is still the envy of the sporting world. As we know over 20 years on it has its critics, but just think about it for a moment. To have the referee hand a decision upstairs to a man who will watch it through, frame-by-frame, and then make the correct call was again ground-breaking. The fact that the replays would be transmitted on a big screen inside the stadium so that the crowds were part and parcel of the process and could see the decisions being made live was a touch of genius. In a stroke they had revolutionised the game.

But they went a step further than that. The players – the gladiators of the game – would be introduced at pitchside by Stevo name by name. They would run out on cue either side of him as he looked down the camera. It would be dramatic to say the least. But as luck would have it, the first time that was put into practice was in Paris on that March night. For a man who regularly mixes up tenses, verbs and nouns in the English language this was to be a challenge to say the least.

Smith and Jones were to be replaced by names like Laurent Lucchese, Mikhail Piskunov, Pierre Chamorin, Arnaud Cervello … I think you can get the drift. This was going to be fraught with danger!

In fact Stevo's starring role might never have happened at all. The bosses at Sky had dug deep and had taken the decision to charter a plane to take us from the UK to Paris for the big kick off. We left way before breakfast time on the morning of the match as there was lots to be done before we finally got on the air later that night. It meant a long day for all concerned.

Stevo had spent much of the journey rehearsing the French players' names. We thought he'd be able to cope with the likes of Matt Crowther, Lynton Stott and Ryan Sheridan from Sheffield. But hang on there was also Waisale Sovatabua and Joe Dakuitoga in the Eagles' line up that night. Good luck old boy!

We got off the plane and headed for the usual passport check and immigration procedures. I was near the back of the line, certain in the knowledge that Stevo was right behind me. I went through passport control and then heard the glass door bang shut behind me and the key turn in the lock. I assumed Stevo must have slipped through earlier than me. No such luck. Maybe it was nerves, maybe the breakfast we'd had on board but Stevo had been taken short and needed the loo. He couldn't wait until he had got through immigration of course. When he emerged from the Gents the room was empty – glass panels from floor to ceiling. The only place that he could possibly get through was above the locked glass door of passport control but even that would be tight.

I must confess I was egging him on: "If you cock your leg over there ... put your foot on there and hoist yourself up there you'll get through," I helpfully suggested. The lad was scaling his own version of Mount Everest when suddenly the door behind him burst open and a burly security guard emerged eyeing him up ... his gun thankfully still safely in its holster. "How is he going to get out of this one?" I thought to myself. Maybe the guard was a rugby league fan, maybe he had somehow seen Stevo on TV. Goodness only knows, but with a wave of the hand he said quite plainly get down. Maybe, just maybe because we had a camera rolling as our journey to France was going to form part of the big build up to kick off, the guard smiled, opened the door and pushed him through. Sky Super League crisis number one (of many) averted!

Sadly we no longer travel to France for the Catalans games. There's now a local TV company in the South of France with the contract to broadcast all the Dragons' home games. We now take the pictures from them and supply our own commentary – generally from Bill Arthur, Barrie McDermott and Terry O'Connor who sit in a little booth in the Sky headquarters in London watching the pictures come in on a small monitor and provide a description of what's happening. A difficult task to say the least from 1,000 miles away. But well done to the lads, they do it brilliantly.

*****

France and our journeys there have produced a few funny stories in the past. It was the norm to charter a plane to take our crew – about 90 of us – from the UK to the South of

France for the games. We headed off early in the morning, returning late at night with a touchdown back home in the early hours of the following day. All glamour this TV lark!

Generally we flew from an airport in the Midlands. Several of our crew are based in the north. Others are based in the south. So to be fair to all parties, Birmingham was the chosen departure point. I remember one morning we'd all arrived at about 4am for the 6am flight and sat in the departure lounge waiting for it to be called. We waited, waited and waited and eventually we were told our departure time was now 12 noon! There were one or two dozen furrowed brows. What the heck was going on?

It later transpired that our plane, a Danube Wings former air force transport plane, had just about limped into Birmingham on the fuel they had on board and of course now they needed to fill up to get us to Perpignan for the game. Only problem was they didn't have a contract with the relevant company at Birmingham and so we were stuck fast. We weren't going anywhere.

The Sky Unit Manager, Kevin Connor, even offered to get the company credit card out and pay for the fuel there and then. But the answer came back that it wasn't possible. Unbeknown to Stevo and me at the time, arrangements were being made to drive us to London to call the game off the monitors. We had sent a skeleton crew out early in case of such an emergency. The pictures could be beamed back to London, although obviously they wouldn't be up to our usual high standards, but at least there would be something to transmit! The kick off was eight o'clock and it was soon not going to be worth the risk of waiting for the argument over the fuel and who would supply it – and more importantly who was going to pay for it – to be resolved.

Eventually the company concerned decided to fill up a tanker at East Midlands Airport where they did have an account and drive it across to us. The fuel duly arrived. Our flight was called and we were herded on to a bus to drive to the plane that was parked somewhere on the outskirts of the airstrip. We arrived and the doors of the bus didn't open. We waited a while then the bus turned round and took us back to the terminal building. You can imagine the uproar on the bus! Turns out because they were re-fuelling, Health and Safety regulations meant we could not get out of the bus or board the plane! Back to the terminal then ... another hour, it was now one o'clock and we were getting a bit panicky but eventually, much to our collective relief, off we went and we landed about five hours late! Fortunately everything in Perpignan went according to plan. Our cameramen, riggers and technical staff did a brilliant job getting everything in place in the nick of time and no one at home was any the wiser.

There was another occasion when we had covered a Great Britain international match against France in Carcassonne on the Wednesday then flew up to Paris for a PSG game on the Friday. We again arrived in the French capital in the early hours and were due to be picked up by a coach and driven to our hotel for the night. We disembarked the plane, wandered through the terminal building and went in search of our transport. We were all shattered and ready for bed as soon as possible. Not even Stevo was interested in a tour of the night-time drinking haunts of Paris so it must have been late!

So where was that bus? There was nothing to be found. A phone call was made to Sarah, the unit manager at the time, who had departed Carcassonne early to make sure the transition went smoothly. "Where's the bus?" was the question.

"It's outside the main terminal building," came the reply. "I'm sitting here looking at the main doors. More to the point where are you lot?"

"We are outside the main doors too and there's no bloody bus!"

Suddenly the penny dropped. We had touched down at Charles de Gaulle airport … Sarah and the coach were positioned outside Orly Airport on the other side of the City! It was eventful going to France for the Super League games to say the least.

There was another time when we all went into the city centre for a spot of lunch before the game. We do have a mobile catering unit for the Super League games here in the UK but no such luxury, of course, in France.

About a dozen of us this particular day set off and found ourselves in a lovely restaurant just across from the Notre Dame Cathedral on the banks of the River Seine. The lunch duly arrived and was consumed with gusto. It was time to pay the bill. I did a quick calculation – there were 11 of us round that table – divided up and with a bit of a tip thrown in it was exactly 50 francs per head (in the days before the Euro). They all threw the notes into the pot and when the waiter returned I was counting them out into his hand. All went well until I dropped a Banque de France cinqante francs note into the palm of his hand. He stopped me putting any more notes on top and shouted: "ILLEGAL, ILLEGAL!' at the top of his voice. Apparently this note had been replaced many months previously and was now no longer legal tender. I looked round and asked who had tried to palm this useless piece of paper off on us? And there was Stevo with his shoulders moving up and down uncontrollably with laughter, although he was blushing bright red to be fair! Apparently he'd been carrying the note around with him for some time and as there were so many others on the plate he believed he could have palmed it off without anyone noticing. Good job the waiter was alert. So he took it back and replaced it with one of the newer notes.

Want to know what happened to that old note? It's in a frame on my desk at home with a caricature of Stevo and me on the top and the note beneath with the words, "You wanted cinquante francs? So here it is. Happy Birthday Eddie". Fancy Stevo going to all that expense for my 50th birthday present! He is generous to a fault!

But back to 1996 and that first ever night in Paris. We got to the ground and the Charléty Stadium was pretty impressive. It had to be rigged though so that cameras, studios, VT operators, commentators and directors were ready to go at the given time, 8pm local. At mid-afternoon we rehearsed the top of the show. At a given moment I was to hand down to Stevo in the players tunnel where he would then announce the names of the 26 men who would be taking to the field to the watching 'millions' back home and the crowd in the stadium via the PA system.

It was a perfect rehearsal. All went smoothly with all the names read – well, almost perfectly. All ready, let's get it on. We adjourned for a bite to eat inside the stadium, Stevo with team lists still in hand going through the names one by one. It all sounded fine. We were all a bit nervous believe me because we were stepping into the unknown. Would we have a crowd? Would there be a video ref call? Do we all know the names of those players? But come the given moment in the live transmission it was Stevo's job to call out the names.

Now what hadn't been rehearsed pre-match and what no one had told us about was that come that moment when Stevo came in vision, the stadium manager would flick a switch and set off a series of firecrackers through which the players would run on to the pitch! So as the players were about to exit the tunnel I said: "So now let's get down to Stevo at pitch-side to introduce the two teams to us on this historic night." And at the same moment that his face appeared in the big screen a switch was pushed somewhere in the stadium and BANG a series of flares and firecrackers went off all round him!

I have never seen someone jump so high and go so pale in an instant. But to his eternal credit, with voice slightly wavering (let's put that down to first night nerves shall we?) off he went with the team sheets.

"Welcome to this historic night in Paris. The teams line up like this (he glares down at his team sheet, swallowing hard): The full back for Paris St Germain is Laurent ... LEN CASEY (it should have been Lucchese with the emphasis on the 'sh'). How Stevo managed to mangle the full back's surname I'll never know. And for those readers who don't know, Len Casey is a former GB international rugby league player who starred in the 70s and 80s!

Anyway Stevo came back to the commentary box looking absolutely shell shocked but hung on in there like the great pro he is and we got through the match in style. The biggest drama came when Stuart Cummings the match referee – who later became a member of the Sky commentary team – called for the first ever video refereeing decision to be made.

I must confess only Nev in the Sky truck knew what was coming. The VT operators and the cameramen were a little in the dark. I think I said that the referee would "now take a look at the big screen" to find out what had gone on in the move leading up to the try. It wasn't quite right but I guess everyone knew what I meant! The first video refereeing decision, for the record, was made ten minutes into the game in Paris by Martin Haigh and it was a decision that denied Paris' Freddie Banquet a try. Stuart Cummings was to ask for two more decisions during that game incidentally, and on both occasions a try was denied to the Sheffield Eagles.

For the record, the first try to be allowed by the new

system came the following night when Martin Offiah was judged to have scored after six minutes of the game against the Oldham Bears at Boundary Park. Even then there was a groan of disbelief from the Boundary Park crowd who thought that Scott Quinell had knocked on in the build-up following a kick from Shaun Edwards!

Video referees were called into action about 90 times during that first season, the most famous being the try that was replayed over and over again concerning St Helens forward Apollo Perilini before he finally got the nod in the game against London Broncos at the Valley. It was a pivotal moment in that first season as the try was awarded and St Helens went on to claim the first ever Super League title by a single point.

But back to that second night of the Super League at Oldham. We had flown home from Paris absolutely buoyant only hours earlier. This was the start of something huge, everyone on board our plane unanimously agreed. Maurice Lindsay's plan was to take the European Super League into the major cities of the continent. Cities like Barcelona and Milan had both been tipped as possible franchises further down the track. With the success in Paris, in front of nearly 18,000 people fresh in our minds, we couldn't go wrong.

Then on Saturday night we hit Oldham! The pre-match entertainment in Paris had been magnificent. The pre-match entertainment in Oldham slightly less so. A Tina Turner look-alike as I remember with a massive hole in her tights! And when Stevo called out the teams in the new fashion (without the flares and the firecrackers I hasten to add), further problems prevailed.

Stevo called out the Wigan team first with the camera on him in front of the dressing room doors this time. Surely nothing would go wrong? So again, just as I had 24 hours earlier in Paris ahead of the game, I gave Stevo his cue to run through the two teams.

"Away team first," he said. "It's Wigan and the full back Kris Radlinski." Radlinski trotted past him. "Next on the wing … it's Martin Offiah." Jason Robinson ran out. Stevo looked perplexed. Undaunted and giving the floor manager, his ex GB international colleague Dave Redfearn who was with him, one of his icy glares he continued: "On the wing it's Martin Offiah." Va'aiga Tuigamala (Inga the Winger) trotted past him.

By now Stevo was just a bit non-plussed but 'Redders' never-the-less gave him the thumbs up and mouthed: "He's coming this time."

Undaunted Stevo carried on: "On the wing it's Martin Offiah." Gary Connolly ran out! By now the crowd were involved and they were cheering every time he got the wrong man. Finally with an air of desperation … and did I detect a little quiver in the voice? "On the wing (gulp) it's Martin Offiah." Finally Chariots actually made his way on to the field. The crowd, and we, all relaxed. They roared their approval. No one had noticed … just one of those things.

As he was making his way round the ground from his position on the far side to our commentary gantry an Oldham fan stopped him and said: "Bloody hell Stevo, we've got no chance tonight!"

"Why is that?" was the reply. "Well they've got five Martin Offiahs playing in their team!" and the guy walked away laughing his head off.

Live TV? Priceless isn't it? And the practice of calling out the players' names by Stevo from the sidelines? It was abandoned very soon after that.

20

Stevo: Lost in France

When the new Super League was born I was up for it big time and what better way to kick off the new era than to fly out for the first ever game in Paris where the Sheffield Eagles were the visitors.

The whole crew were excited and we met up in Manchester Airport for a special chartered flight – all the cameramen, technicians, the lot – we couldn't believe this was happening.

I had flown into England from Sydney only two days before and was still jet-lagged from the flights, but I was eager to get on the plane to Paris. It was so good to meet up again with all the crew, especially Marion, one of our assistant editors. Marion was a real character – a stick-thin, purple Doc Marten wearing, alternative music loving, vegetarian communist. In fact her views on communism were so forthright that I often wondered if she wouldn't have been happier living in Russia.

She was good at her job though and my mind went back to the day we were shooting a piece for *Boots 'n' all* where Dewsbury Town Council had named a road after me in recognition of my days as a player at Dewsbury. They had built a new housing project on the old Crown Flatt ground which had burnt down a couple of years earlier. In a tribute to several stalwarts from the old club they'd created Waring

Way (after Eddie Waring, the former Dewsbury manager and great BBC commentator), Coates Close (in recognition of Henry Coates, the last surviving member of the 1929 Wembley team) and Stephenson Close.

Obviously I was proud as punch and looked it when we tried to film the section where I pointed to the Stephenson Close street sign, only for Marion to interrupt and shout out it was typical that they had named it on a dead-end street. By the time she and the cameraman stopped laughing, the bloke who owned the house and the wall where the sign was mounted came out and told us all to sod off and stop filming his garden!

So our meeting again at the airport was enjoyable, especially when I saw she had dyed her hair bright orange. What made matters worse, she had socks on to match (and the faithful purple Doc's).

"Bloody hell, Marion … did you have any left in the bottle to dye the growler?"

Amazingly everyone laughed except for Marion who gave me a look that would have made Stalin shiver and a mouthful which can't be repeated here!

Marion was soon laughing though when I was bursting for a pee after we had got off the plane in Paris. Eddie has explained my problem in detail where I came out from the toilet in the immigration hall to find everyone had gone through passport control and the officials had locked up and gone away.

I was stranded in no man's land and Marion and the others were howling their socks off at my predicament and shouting loudly that someone was trying to get into France without a passport. I was halfway over the glass partition when an armed guard pointed his gun at me and motioned for me to get down. I don't speak much French but I got the gist quickly. It took ages to sort out but I got through in the end, much to the amusement of everyone in the luggage hall.

Things got even more confusing when we all filed out to what should have been the waiting coach to take us the Charléty Stadium where the new Paris St Germaine rugby league side were playing. It was running late and we were all getting a touch nervy.

We arrived into the stadium hungry and tired hoping for a good lunch only to find someone had forgotten to arrange catering, so Eddie and I quickly trotted across the road from the stadium to a good old fashioned French bistro where we delighted in ordering steak and pommes frites. Others just grabbed what they could and some of the cameramen surprised us by not bothering to eat at all. They felt comfortable to share a few bottles of red instead.

Eddie again has detailed about me calling the names of the French side just before kick off when nobody informed me where or when the fireworks would go off. Putting it mildly, I crapped myself and made a right cotton balls of it. And what made matters worse was I had given the Sheffield team sheet to the French announcer. On our team sheets the names are written with the surname first and then the christian name, so all the supporters heard things like Senior-Keith, Ashton-Mark and so on. To say it was a shambles was an understatement, yet the fireworks nearly did a good job of ruining my suit trousers (not to mention my boxer shorts). I was surprised I didn't find a spent Catherine wheel in my pocket when it ended!

PSG won that night and we were out on our feet when we got back to the hotel, feeling knackered but exhilarated about the new era and the game watched by over 17,000 fans. We were up and running and Europe was at our feet.

What we didn't know at the time was that a supermarket chain had given away free tickets for the match to French customers if they purchased a certain amount over the counter. This pissed off the few Sheffield supporters who had to pay full entry price for the game as well as the cost of getting to Paris in the first place. But I'm sure they remember it now with much pride having watched history being made.

Calling the game in Paris made for such a great trip which we enjoyed for a few years before PSG finally hit the rocks. Thankfully Catalans took up the mantle in the South of France and that too has been a great treat to travel to and broadcast from in the land of the croissant

We had some great matches as well as plenty of laughs at the Stade Sébastien in Charléty, Paris, although one incident inside the stadium led to one of the crew being ordered back to the UK in disgrace. Bob was his name and sadly he is no longer with us, but on this day he was helping set up the equipment for counting the stats, tackles, runs from dummy-half and that sort of thing when he saw his statistician colleague being told by a French official that he had to walk all the way to the other side of the pitch before trying to get upstairs. Poor Bob shouted out far too loudly: "Tell the bloody frog to stick his head up his arse and come up the wrong (but shorter) way." He didn't realise the French official had a better knowledge of the English language than I have and demanded poor Bob leave the stadium otherwise no broadcast would be forthcoming!

Neville had no option but to send Bob off to the airport and we never saw him again.

Another French airport drama came the year after that first Paris match, only this time instead of the transfer bus being late it just wasn't there, despite having an assistant producer come out the day before to ensure everything went smoothly. I forget her name – which perhaps is a Godsend!

After waiting over one hour and making several phone

calls to her we still didn't have a bus but she kept insisting she and the bus were parked outside terminal two. It suddenly dawned on Nev to ask her the obvious question: "Which airport are you at?" to which she replied: "Orly," only we were stood outside Charles de Gaulle!

We all rushed to grab taxis to the stadium and got there with just enough time to prepare for the match. That same evening after the game we were in the lounge having a few drinks when I noticed a package on the floor next to where this same girl had been sitting and had just gone to bed. Being a nosey bugger I walked over and to my surprise found an envelope with over 3,000 francs inside to pay for the hotel bill. However, the next morning when I saw her at breakfast I asked if she was missing anything. She said no!

The hotel did get paid but the fun and games didn't stop there when a few months later she had ordered not just one high lifter for the overhead camera but four. Nev was far from impressed but it all had to come to an end when at one of the grounds the stadium floodlights went out before we could do the after-game interviews. Neville screamed out loud to her: "Get the bloody lights back on NOW," at which she proceeded to turn on the lights in the studio truck! I believe her P45 was in the post the next day.

*****

It wasn't just in this country that the fun and games continued. On one trip to Australia there was a gap between the last Test in Brisbane and the series in New Zealand, so Eddie, Nev and I decided we would spend a week in Fiji.

I'd been before and knew what a relaxing place the Islands were – so laid back it was nearly horizontal. In the entire world Fiji is the one place you can fall asleep waiting for anything, and I mean anything – beer, ice cream, cocktail, a bus, a taxi. The country moves at a very sedate speed.

I convinced them to go to a lovely resort on the south coast about 20 miles from Suva where I had visited a few years earlier. Nev was single in those days and was keen to know if they had a disco and good bar. "Mate it's all action," I replied.

After landing we looked for our connection to take us to the resort and watched as all the other tourists boarded luxury air conditioned coaches that left pretty quickly, only to leave one decrepit looking charabanc with no glass in the windows that was built well before the Second World War.

Neville was peeved, Eddie wasn't too impressed either and after travelling at about 15 mph, this death trap finally pulled up outside the resort at about five minutes after midnight. "The lad's trying his best," I remarked to my two irritated friends at the slow pace the driver was making, and to be fair we were safer at a 'pedestrian' speed as any faster might have seen the thing collapse.

We signed in and were greeted by the usual welcome of 'Bula Vinaka' and given some mango juice, which was warm, so off to the bar we went.

The bar was empty and there were no staff but a long shouting session eventually attracted the attention of a large lady dressed in a local floral dress. Again we were greeted with 'Bula Vinaka'. We ordered three large beers and 15 minutes later they arrived! So we ordered another three straight away and that's how it was all week.

Neville now was eager to see the disco upstairs, so we dragged ourselves up there to find that empty too – no music, nothing! I could tell Nev wasn't too pleased but thankfully I found a set of carpet bowls in a cupboard where we spent three hours drinking (slowly) and finding out if it was better to go thumb or finger on the bowls. Eventually we crashed out in our sumptuous rooms where I slept well, so did Eddie but Nev tossed and turned irritated to the hilt and no doubt dreaming of ABBA singing 'Dancing Queen'.

Neville was surprised to see me down at the pool just after 8am with what he thought was orange juice in my glass. He took a gulp and nearly choked. "It's got vodka in it!"

"I know, we are on holiday."

The hotel was great, with a big swimming pool and right by a sandy beach with a reef where fish swam around your feet. They also had a restaurant built on the edge of the reef and you had to wade through a foot of warm water to get there. It served fantastic food – fresh fish, good beer and wine – and they had candles on the wooden tables to emphasise the romance for all the tourists that were on honeymoon. But it never worked for me. I like Eddie and Nev but not that much!

The only problem with the restaurant is that it didn't have a loo. You had to walk back to the main building for that and I certainly wasn't prepared to walk so far just for a pee. Anyway I wouldn't have made it. So I decided to relieve myself just outside away onto the reef side. Little did I know that you could see my shadow clearly from the inside and amazingly the flow of my urine. It didn't go down too well with the lovebirds smooching across the tables and probably the fish were somewhat disturbed too!

We dined in the main building after that.

Despite a few mishaps it was great to have a break, even though we flew into Auckland five days before we had to work when Neville decided living with Eddie and me had taken its toll.

"No offence but I've just booked a three day skiing holiday in the mountains." Adios Amigo!

I don't ski, and I don't think Eddie does but we enjoyed touring Auckland which had changed a lot since I first went there in 1973. Back then I'd arrived on a cruise ship on a Sunday and found nothing open – no shops, no café, no pub, no club, NOTHING!

Things had changed and the New Zealand dollar was so weak against the British pound that we lived it up big time. Pubs, clubs and restaurants were doing great business and each morning we would walk across the road to one of the oldest swimming pools in the world where we swam away our jet lag (ok, hangover).

We were pleased to see Neville back at the hotel after his skiing break and wondered what tales he had to tell. The first one said it all, he had failed to realise why the trip was such good value until he arrived and found out it was organised by a church group with no alcohol at the resort.

We left him to get over it whilst Eddie and I argued about which restaurant we should have lunch at and waited to see if Nev had turned religious or not.

21

Eddie: The Super League Years

March 29th, 1996, was the day that the European Super League was born. A seismic shift for the game moving from winter to summer. A moment in history and one that has given the greatest game its greatest leg up. So many memories from that first night in Paris to Old Trafford, Australia, New Zealand and beyond. Over 20 years … great games and great personalities.

Way back in 1996 Wigan were the dominant force in the game. No one could touch them. Champions seven years in a row, Challenge Cup winners eight years in a row. It was getting just a bit boring for everyone outside the Wigan Borough. The time for change had come, new names were needed on the game's honours list. Since then the Leeds Rhinos, St Helens, Bradford Bulls and Warrington Wolves have had their days in the sun. Yes nicknames for teams also came in during 1996 to give the sport a fresh look.

Catalans Dragons have, over ten years, lit a flame in the south of France. Castleford Tigers and Widnes Vikings have emerged as possible future champions. Would all this have happened without the emergence of the Super League? We would never have seen full-time professional players or the new stadia teams are playing in now that's for sure.

In 1996 St Helens emerged from Wigan's shadow and under Shaun McRae's coaching they won the League and

Cup double. The following season Bradford Bulls lit up the Super League with an expansive brand of rugby league and show stopping pre-match entertainment that really was the envy of the Sporting World. Then in 1998 came the first play-off system and the Grand Final under lights at the Theatre of Dreams – Old Trafford the home of Manchester United. A concept that has taken rugby league to new heights and that now completely dwarfs – for all its history, pomp, ceremony and tradition – the Challenge Cup Final at Wembley.

We would never have had the Magic Weekend, where the game is showcased around the country with all the teams playing a full round of matches over one glorious weekend, back-to-back inside one stadium. Cardiff, Edinburgh, Manchester and Newcastle have all enjoyed the arrival of 70-odd thousand rugby league fans filling their pubs, clubs and restaurants and pouring millions of pounds into their local coffers.

Would we have seen on a regular basis the top teams from Australia's NRL tangling with the best that Super League has to offer in a World Club Championship weekend? I very much doubt it. Rugby League, or Super League as it is now universally known, has grown and gained respect from a myriad of other sports for its bravery, athleticism and skill like never before. Stars like Wayne Rooney and Joey Barton from the Premier League are regularly to be found on social media eulogising about one of the greatest televised sports they've ever seen.

And on a purely personal note, we would never have had the now famous "Wide to West try" from the play offs of 2000. Allow me to expand.

The Bradford Bulls were playing St Helens in the qualifying play-offs at the old and wonderful Knowsley Road ground for the right to move a step closer to Old Trafford and the Grand Final that year. We had reached the dying seconds of the game and Bradford were clinging on to a slender lead and on their way to the semi-finals the following week where they would have played Wigan for the right to walk out at the Theatre of Dreams.

What transpired that night is now the stuff of rugby league folklore and, if I may be so bold was the greatest moment in the history of the Super League so far. Stevo and I were lucky enough to be behind the microphone. It was a fantastic contest. We had reached the closing minute and Saints looked dead and buried. Bradford were going to make progress and take a perceived easier route (just one more game) to make it to the big night.

What happened next has flatteringly been described as rugby league's equivalent to Kenneth Wolstenholme's 'They think it's all over ... It is now' commentary in the 1966 soccer World Cup Final at Wembley. Unlike that incredible moment for Wolstenholme, my 'Wide to West try' commentary has been reproduced on the wall of Saints' new Langtree Park stadium, printed on thousands of T-shirts and even local choirs have composed songs about it incorporating all the words that were used.

For the record Bradford were leading 11-10 as the game reached the last 60 seconds and this is how the drama unfolded:

Eddie: "West is tackled by Vaikona ... and over the line! That's the match ... that's going to be the match for Bradford."

Stevo: "He's given a penalty."

Eddie: "Oh he has!"

Stevo: "He called held there. They (Saints) are still not out of it. They've taken a short one, they know they've got only ten seconds left. Will they get the play the ball? They're holding him down."

('Him' was Paul Sculthorpe who had been tackled by

three Bradford players who did their best to keep him on the ground until the siren sounded. Sculthorpe shoved them off him, played the ball and so it happened.)

Eddie: "Sculthorpe wants to get on with it … Bradford fans are counting down. This is the last play the ball … Long kicks it wide to Iro … Iro to Hall … Hall is trapped … back it goes to Hoppe ... over the shoulder to Hall … there is Jonkers … here is Long … and Long fancies it … Long fancies it ... it's wide to West … it's wide to West ... Dwayne West … inside to Joynt … Joy-nt … Jo-yn-t … Oh! Oh! Fantastic … they've won it. They've won it. Chris Joynt has won it. It's unbelievable here, frankly unbelievable. What a try. What a match. What drama!"

And so there you have it. It doesn't look much in hard print does it? But reading it and watching it now, even to this day I still get a shiver down my back and the hairs stand up on my neck. It was a moment when the crib sheet we prepare ahead of the game simply goes out of the window and you speak from the heart. The poor old Bradford coach Mathew Elliott couldn't believe what he had just seen (frankly none of us inside the ground that night could) and Matty went to sit back down on his seat holding his head in his hands. But the old stand at Knowsley Road had flip-up seats and Matty ended up on the floor!

The final scene in the drama came next. Sean Long, the iconic St Helens scrum half, picked up the costume head of the Saints mascot St Bernard as he prepared to take the conversion! Pure theatre and a memory that will last with me until my dying day.

*****

Thanks to Super League because we would never have had moments like that Wide to West try. And thanks to Super

League again because we also would never have had the quips and sayings of Stevo sitting alongside me. Some priceless unforgettable broadcasting moments. Probably too many to remember but those I vividly recalled are printed here for posterity:

Me: "You know Stevo, Saints have dropped the ball with the line at their mercy tonight at least six times."

Stevo: "Oh no Eddie, I'd put it much higher than that. It must be into double figures now. Saints have dropped the ball NINE times!"

Stevo (when ex-Leeds and Warrington prop forward Adrian Morley flew into one of his trademark tackles): "Adrian Morley hit him with all the force of an EXERCISE missile!"

Stevo (once when a player dropped the ball when over the try line and seemed certain to score): "The wheel is turning but the hamster has left the cage!"

Stevo: "This guy is ad-MIRE-able."

Me: "Ad-Mire-able eh? Well that's Spec-TACKLE!"

Stevo (as Quentin Pongia of Wigan and Danny Ward of Leeds went head to head during a spot of bother on the pitch): "What animal mates like that?"

Stevo (about Luke Robinson the former Wigan, Castleford and Huddersfield scrum half): "Twinkle twinkle – he's a star!"

Stevo: "It's like buying a ticket to see the Three Tenors and Russ Conway comes out!" (About a mistake that had just happened on the field.)

Stevo: "I've never really got it (after a mistake from a Wakefield knock on), I need to see a psychiatrist."

Producer Nev (down the headphones to all the crew therefore not public until this moment): "Who'd like Stevo to see a psychiatrist?"

Stevo: "This is all the fun of the fair isn't it – just knock his head off!"

Stevo: "Ian Millward (St Helens coach) has gone straight to the dressing rooms to check on his big prop."

Nev (again to the entire crew on the talk back button): "Is that what he calls it?"

Stevo: It's as though he sent a telegram to him. I'm stood here ... send it to me!"

Stevo: (proving spelling is not his strongest subject): "It's a G.A.P. for a T.A.R.Y!"

But perhaps Stevo's finest moment behind the mic came when we were covering a match at Huddersfield. Bobbie Goulding the former Great Britain scrum half was involved, and in the papers on the morning of the match Bobbie had decided that despite his England allegiances he had declared that he would like to play for Wales in the upcoming World Cup tournament. During a long break in play because of an injury we'd just about run out of things to say when that fact popped into my head.

Me: "I see Bobbie Goulding has elected to play for Wales Stevo in the up-coming World Cup."

Stevo: "Och aye the noo Eddie."

Me: "So that's och aye the noo boyo then is it?"

Great memories, great fun. What a way to earn a living!

22

Eddie: Health Blues

I think by now you might have gathered it has been wonderful and the best of times working for Sky for 30 years.

Our team – and I mean Stevo, Nev and me – have been together almost since day one. We've certainly shared every memory of the Super League and a few before that in the Big League days when we covered the old First Division Championship. Between us we have only missed a handful of games because of sickness or bereavements. And all three of us sadly have suffered those.

In later years we have had ex-players Phil Clarke, Brian Carney, Terry O'Connor, Barrie McDermott and Jon Wells working alongside us – all of them doing a sterling job in their own right. Reporters Bill Arthur and Angela Powers have been there for a good long while as well. And it's not just in front of the camera that people can boast about their longevity of service. There haven't been many changes down the years and the reason for that is that the rugby league team at Sky has always been seen as one of the happiest and most settled. Generally it has been regarded as a good team to work with. Obviously that comes down to the way we all work together. There haven't been that many rows or tantrums.

Nev of course is an ex cameraman and I well remember

his words of wisdom early on: "Get to know the guys behind those cameras, the lighting engineers and the sound men. If you fall out with them they can make or break you." It was terrific advice. We don't have 'stars' in the rugby league department. We all get on very well together. You have to of course when you're transmitting over 100 live games a year.

The guys pointing those lenses at you can make you look very silly at times, such as the day we were in Dublin to cover the Charity Shield Final between Wigan and Leeds in 1995. The game was to be played at the Royal Dublin Showground just 24 hours after a huge horse show had been staged there. They were still clearing the pitch of some manure when we actually got there!

The arena had been dressed for the occasion the day before and there were hanging baskets filled with flowers all over the place. Just before we went on air, the cameraman who was looking after the main studio area asked Stevo to move just a few feet to his left. There wasn't much room on the TV gantry so we knew there must be a very good reason for the request.

I looked down at the TV monitor we had set up in the presentation area and realised immediately what a good call it was. Had he stayed in his original position, Stevo would have had two hanging baskets immediately behind his head. And as they were hanging off the roof of the stand in the distance, had he not been moved it would have appeared that he had a pair of flowery earrings for the full length of the programme! The cameraman saved all of his blushes ... though I must say when I saw the shot of him, he did look quite fetching with red geraniums hanging off each ear!

So we are a great team and we all feel the pain when one of us suffers the loss of a parent, is off ill or there is some domestic crisis that might need sorting out. We all pull together to paper over the crack and carry on regardless of troubles that might be evident elsewhere. You have to liken the role of frontman to that of a swan swimming on the water. All looks serene and majestic above the surface. Below it you're paddling away furiously just trying to keep afloat!

Fortunately we haven't had too many of these incidents in all the years we've been together and, even if I do say so myself, we've all remained pretty healthy down the years too. Every time Stevo comes back from Australia, though, for the start of the season in late January – having left the heat and sunshine of Sydney behind him and dropping into the cold English winter – he has often been dogged by chest infections.

Generally he has coughed and spluttered his way through things. We always tell him to rest his voice a bit during the games and let some of the others in a bit more often and it has worked a treat. But things were very different at the start of the 2015 season.

He contracted a shocking dose of pleurisy and had to be hospitalised because the antibiotics he usually takes simply weren't working. He missed six weeks of that campaign and was really ill. And I must confess I missed him. You see having worked together all these years we have of course developed a rapport. It's always been good cop/bad cop. I call the names and Stevo makes the critical and controversial points. But we know each other so well. I'll take a pause, Stevo will come in with a comment and unless something dramatic develops on the field I know exactly when he has finished and I'll pick it up again.

But what happened in 2016 was awful for him.

Stevo had returned to the UK limping and being supported by a walking stick. He had been told he would need a hip replacement and so for the first three months of the season he was completely out of action while a surgeon in London (the best in the world according to Stevo) did his job. Apparently, when he'd first begun his playing career in the 1960s and he'd just broken into the England Under-23 team, he'd been told that the rigours of playing rugby league with a dodgy back would maybe come to haunt him later on. How right could that diagnosis have been? He played for much of his professional career wearing a steel support to his back, a corset he told me. And there I was thinking for all these years he'd been wearing a corset on a rugby field purely and simply because his wife had found it in the back of his car!

So for six weeks in 2015, and three months in 2016, Stevo, my safety net, simply wasn't there. I confess to you now I felt like I'd lost an arm. Of course as far as the viewers were concerned they were either unaware ... or delighted with the change. You see you either love him or hate him. It's as simple as that!

I remember one year he came round the corner in Cardiff and came face to face with a group of fans on their way to the Millennium Magic games of the weekend and all of them stopped in their tracks. "Stevo, is that you?" one of them said. "There's a report this morning that you had died ... are you sure that's you?" Social media you see – what a curse. It had my old mate dead and buried!

As Mark Twain stated all those years ago, the reports of his death had been greatly exaggerated! He has his critics – there are many of them – but once Stevo hangs up the microphone for good, believe me, there will be thousands of people who quite rightly will say that things will never be the same again. He will be appreciated more when he's not there than now when he is and I for one wish that day will never come but sadly we all know that it will.

There was another year, right at the start of the Super League era, and Stevo wasn't well at all. He had been suffering from stomach pains for a good while. I remember vividly we were at Boundary Park, the home of the Oldham Bears, and he was a dreadful colour and doubled up in pain. Somehow he got through the match. He's a tough old boy is Stevo and we realised just how tough when we all found out the next day he'd been admitted to hospital for an emergency operation to remove his gallbladder which had grown to the size of a grapefruit!

I left it a day or two before going in to see him in his hospital bed. He was in the Salford Royal and I was ushered into his room. There he was in all his glory! I'd done the right thing – you always buy grapes for the sick don't you? Plus I'd taken him in a half dozen cans of Guinness to aid his way to recovery (when the surgeons allowed of course).

He didn't look well at all. He was exhausted but at least his spirits were up. I'd been there for about half an hour or so and he was starting to drop off to sleep, so I said I'd leave him to it and come back and see him again. I shook his hand when he asked me to pass him the disposable urinal from the top of his locker.

Gingerly I picked it up and gave it to him. No escape now I thought to myself. I suppose I'll have to dispose of this before I go. He took the bottle from me, lifted the sheet and looked down. As he did so he uttered the words, in a broad Yorkshire accent: "Eh … the poor lad doesn't know what's hit him!" We both shrieked with laughter (maybe his was more pain than laughter, I don't know) but he did what he had to do and then passed the bottle over the top of the sheet for me to get rid of. The things you do for your mates!

*****

Personally I've been lucky enough to remain pretty healthy over the years and, apart from the odd cough and cold, I can't remember too many days off work. When Carole's dear dad and then mum passed away, and then in 2014 my own dad left us, I did take some time off but health wise things haven't gone too badly.

That was of course until the spring of 2013 when, after a purely routine blood test, it was discovered I had developed prostate cancer. I say the blood test was routine, it certainly was. I was in the GP surgery for something totally mundane when he looked at his computer and said I hadn't had a full blood test for several years. My doctor, Andrew Beare-Winter, made the appointment for me and it was then that the trouble started.

My PSA (prostate-specific antigen) levels were a bit high and so I was sent off for further tests, examinations, scans and biopsies which at the end of a couple of months produced the dreaded words from my urologist Paul Jameson: "This is the part of my job that's not nice. I have to tell you Eddie you have prostate cancer!"

You could have knocked me down with a feather. There were no symptoms – nothing. I was only 63 for goodness sake. This couldn't possibly be true. The good news was it was in its very early stages, was one of the non-aggressive types and had not broken out of the gland. All good news really. I was told to go away, read the literature I was now being given (strangely entitled the Tool Kit!) and then come back and let them know what I would like to do about it.

It was at this time I met my oncologist, Dr. Shaun Tolan, and another meeting was arranged with a surgeon to see what route my treatment should take. I was in a bit of a haze really. I read the first article of the Tool Kit and frightened myself to death. I had been told it was the non-aggressive and early stage of the cancer so I could do nothing but

169

watch and wait, which sounded pretty good to me being the coward that I am. Initially I decided that was the course of action I would take. I'd watch and wait and see.

I told only the immediate family of my diagnosis originally. My kids Lisa, Sharon and Mark were all pretty worried by now but I told myself I had to stay positive and think only good things. Carole and I would be facing this together but I think we sort of pushed it to the back of our minds. You know the feeling, if you don't think or talk about it, it just might go away!

Obviously, as so many of the tests I was having would be running through the weeks of the rugby league season, I had to make work aware of my situation. Nev was the first port of call. He's now one of my closest friends and he was clearly upset but he assured me that he would do anything that was needed to help me get through it all as far as work was concerned. This was confirmed too by Barney Francis, the Head of Sky Sports. I couldn't believe how kind people were being. The next person who needed telling, quietly, because you don't want news like this being talked about every time you turn up for work, was my old mate Stevo.

I remember the day vividly. We were at Castleford Tigers for a game that night. I needed a quiet word with him I said, and so a couple of hours before we went on air we wandered up to the TV gantry where it was all peace and quiet. I told Stevo I'd received the news that week that I had prostate cancer but that it was first stage, non-aggressive and confined. I know we are close – he's always called me 'Top Man' and I love him to bits too – but on hearing the news he virtually collapsed into my arms and his legs gave way. He said: "Oh no … not you Top Man … anyone but you. It can't be true." We both had to use our hankies for a moment or two but we recovered our composure. I convinced him I'd be fine (I wasn't totally convinced myself at this stage to be fair) and I wouldn't be going anywhere soon. I was watching and waiting!

Watching and waiting sounded the easy way out of course. No action required just more tests and maybe biopsies further down the line. But it's incredible what hearing that word 'cancer' does to you. Last thing at night as I closed my eyes to go to sleep my only thought was, "damn I've got cancer" and on waking up the following morning the first thing into my head was, "damn I've got cancer".

So it didn't take long before Carole and I decided that further action was required. I have to say here also that my colleague, Bill Arthur, was the most incredible help and support to me throughout this whole procedure. Bill himself had been diagnosed some 18 months before me so had been through the whole process. He was undergoing treatment himself at the time and probably the last thing he really wanted to do when he saw me was to talk about prostate cancer. We did mostly steer clear of it but the odd time I needed reassurance and encouragement about what was to come, Bill was there for me. I'd like to thank Bill publicly now for all his help, encouragement and kind words. I would have struggled to get by without him.

The big problem was what to do about it. I was lucky in a way as I had been caught early so I had a number of options open to me. Dr. Tolan – who is now Shaun to me and I am Eddie to him and we have developed a great relationship – was in favour of either brachytherapy or radiotherapy. They were his special fields. I had ruled out surgery a long time ago. So in the end, after much soul searching and research, I elected for radiotherapy under Shaun's watchful eye with his team of radiotherapists at the Clatterbridge Cancer Centre on the Wirral.

Shaun is a great rugby league fan himself – well he supports St Helens! – so I found we were talking Super

171

League for 60 per cent of the time I was with him and prostate cancer for 40 per cent, which was absolutely fine by me. Shaun and his team at Clatterbridge I think, hope and pray, have worked miracles.

My first PSA reading on Valentine's Day, 2013, stood at 7.6. Two months later it had risen to 8.6 which was when we thought further action should be taken. In August it was down to 7.0 and then I embarked on a series of hormone treatments to get me ready for the radiotherapy that was to begin that December.

We had stepped off a plane from Florida on the morning of December 8th, 2013, having just arrived back from a fabulous two weeks in the sunshine and I got straight down to the business of the 32 sessions I needed to get rid of this terrible disease. The two brilliant radiologists who looked after me throughout my Clatterbridge experience – Sarah-Jane and Lois – plonked me on the machine and the journey began. Just before the 2014 season got under way it was all over.

The first PSA reading after the treatment was on February 24th, 2014, (Carole's birthday coincidentally!) and the reading was 0.1. The miracle had happened, and the reading has hovered around 0.2-0.3 ever since. The team at Clatterbridge were so impressive that I wanted to put something back if I could, so I asked how I could go about that. I am now one of their ambassadors for the Cancer Centre and I am happily involved in fundraising for them ahead of a move to the brand new Royal Liverpool Teaching Hospital which is costing millions. Hopefully they have saved my life and although Shaun still says to this day: "Well so far so good!" it is the very least I can do.

The moral of this story? Well if you are a man in the over-60 age group and/or you have history of prostate cancer in your immediate family, please, please go and get yourself checked out. OK, it's not very dignified at times, but what would you rather do? Spare a few blushes and potentially fall foul of this dreadful, silent killer? Please heed the warning and put trust in the remarkable, wonderful professionals who deal with the trials and tribulations of cancer on a daily basis. It's a no-brainer I think you'll agree.

23

Stevo: John Kear, a Bowl of Rice and a Surfboard

As you may have gathered whilst reading through this book we have both had some funny moments and I certainly want to bring out a few nuggets that raised an eyebrow or created a laugh.

Quite a few have been in France, on trips to watch either PSG, Catalans Dragons or England taking on the French national side. One bizarre moment came about in the central square in Carcassone on the Saturday before England took on France at the Stade Albert Domec.

Eddie, Neville and yours truly decided to have a slap-up lunch in one of the trendy restaurants in the square and as soon as we walked through the door the lady who owned the joint came rushing across and hugged me! I had never seen her before in my life yet she started showering kisses at me and shouting: "Anglaise, Anglaise", smiled at me and shouted to the waiter to seat us in a nice corner near the window.

Eddie and Nev were flabbergasted and I just couldn't understand the big welcome and all the fuss.

Nev said: "She obviously watches Sky Sports and has recognised you," Eddie quickly added: "Do they get Sky down here? I've not seen any dishes in the town."

Either way we had a most delightful lunch and the

hostess kept bringing out bottles of top quality wine for our consumption.

It was now late in the afternoon and we knew we had a game to call the following day, so despite this lady trying to force even more wine down our throats, we finally made our way to the door. To our surprise she wouldn't let us pay the bill, which was so nice, and this time it was our turn to offer kisses either side of the cheek. Yet before we could get out of the door, she raced back into the kitchen to come out with the local newspaper which had a nice article about England and a photo of the Coach John Kear!

"Please you must sign for me," she said.

So I did with a bold flourish: "Best wishes, John Kear".

A few weeks later I had the great pleasure of informing Mr Kear, who has a reputation of never having a wallet or paying his round. He was miffed that he missed out and to this day claims I owe him lunch!

Oh the joys of being attractive!

*****

Carcassonne is a lovely place with an impressive fortress and castellated walls that overlook and surround the old city. It's a great place to visit with quaint streets and some nice restaurants too. I think it was our second visit to 'Le Cité' when a group of eight Sky guys joined us for dinner where I encouraged them to have the local dish, cassoulet, a stew made with haricot beans, pork, mutton and sausages.

The waiter asked everyone for their order and it went round the table like this: "Cassoulet please," "cassoulet thank you," ... until it got round to me. "I will have the duck." Eddie quickly smelled a rat and ordered duck too.

What the others didn't know is that Cassoulet is a very hearty meal, usually served in the winter when it's cold.

175

After about ten minutes of pushing this local stew around his bowl, Bill Arthur said: "I think mine's growing!"

They've never forgiven me for that piece of advice.

*****

Another restaurant, this time in London, proved to be a bit too much for a certain lady who was given the job of advising both Eddie and me what type of clothing we should wear on screen. She was a fashion stylist and ensured we didn't buy clashing colours, had different ties, the job lot. We certainly enjoyed these trips out to the top stores in Bond Street where we were fussed over and looked after by sales staff to ensure we would look our best on TV.

On the day, the lady in question arrived a bit late and when she finally got there you could tell she was a touch flustered and in full sweat mode.

"You look like you've come on a bike," I said.

"I have, sorry I'm late, it took a while to find somewhere to chain my bike."

Evidently she had lost her driving licence for speeding, hence the pushbike.

The shopping went fine and seeing as both Eddie and I were going to the launch of the new season that night at a sports bar near Leicester Square we invited her to join us. As time was running out, she decided to give the bike a miss and catch a tube so she could get changed and be back in time for the function that night.

It proved to be a wonderful evening, so much so that Chris Caisley, the Super League boss, invited us to join him in China Town for a late dinner.

So about ten of us found ourselves sitting at a huge, round table with one of those spinning centrepieces full of exotic food – lemon chicken, pork with ginger, prawns, noodles, boiled rice, fried rice – so much that it made the table groan.

Beer and wine flowed, much to the delight of us all. But our stylist was struggling with the pace and the drink. She was fading fast when suddenly her head dropped into the huge bowl of boiled rice as she passed out. Seeing as we were only halfway through the meal we didn't want to disturb her, so I carefully lifted her head out of the rice to serve myself a portion then gently lowered her back into the bowl again. Not surprisingly the fried rice became very popular after that.

We all agreed what gentlemen we were in not disturbing her beauty sleep until we had finished eating when we eventually guided her into a taxi to take her home.

I received a phone call early the following morning as she wanted to know if I knew where she had chained her pushbike. Sadly she never found it and I have never had boiled rice since.

*****

One of the many honours Eddie and I have enjoyed was when we were asked to host a Rugby League Centenary show at the world famous Leeds City Varieties. This great theatre has seen the likes of Charlie Chaplin, Houdini and Morecambe and Wise take to the stage and we were overwhelmed to be asked to emulate the famous *Good Old Days* show that had been brilliantly compered by the actor Leonard Sachs.

We arrived in Leeds three hours before the show to be enthusiastically greeted by the producer: "How wonderful to have such talent on the show. I just know it's going to be a huge success, especially with John Inman the star tonight."

We both looked at each other, our faces not showing the same enthusiasm as the producer who then asked: "Right, where is your script?"

"Script?" we both spouted out (Eddie and I have ad-libbed for over 25 years).

"Oh no. you don't have a script do you? This show will be ruined!" he said and left the stage in anguish.

Over a few pints in the pub next door we somehow produced a 'script' that got us through the evening and made for an enjoyable event.

Charlie Chaplin must have turned in his grave.

*****

The Sky rugby league team has a big motorhome we use for meetings, relaxing and a make-up room before we go on air. It's produced some classic moments and perhaps the best was at Hull FC's old ground, the Boulevard, where one of our female assistant producers had that morning gone for a swim at the hotel pool and decided to leave her bikini to dry in the motor home shower area.

It was a chance not to be missed and whilst she was doing a facilities check in the outside scanner studio, I quickly stripped to my undies and put the thing on which came as a big surprise to her when she returned.

I can't repeat what she said when she opened the door to find me standing there, looking quite cute if you must know, although perhaps the socks didn't help.

She went ape shit, so I thought it wise to take it off quickly. But it didn't help much when I said: "Look, it fits me like a glove!"

Two hours later there was a smell of smoke out in the car park where she was 'burning' her bikini. I have called her 'Large Bottom' ever since. Please don't ask what she calls me!

*****

Going overseas can be a bit daunting for anyone, especially for some of the younger staff we have at Sky. And for two guys who still work with us, Steve Owen and Ben Proe, it proved costly when both decided to take in food to New Zealand. Steve had a sandwich and Ben had an apple and they tried to get past immigration which is a no-no for the land of the big white cloud and a hefty 200 dollar fine had to be paid on the spot!

Australasia is wonderful and I'm looking forward to spending more time in my home in Sydney and making a few trips to New Zealand as well. The best way to see New Zealand is by cruise ship and I love Auckland where Eddie and I have had such great times over there calling tour games and World Cup matches. It's a great city to relax in and the people are fantastic, they make you so welcome. However, they don't hang back with a few choice words – especially on radio.

The bald and long nose duo were invited to do a live interview down at a lovely restaurant on the harbour side in Auckland where the first remark on air about rugby league threw both of us off track when the interviewer said: "… the England squad is crap and you have shit forwards!"

We looked at each other in amazement wondering how they could get away with such remarks. Bizarrely things proceeded to get even worse as the interview went on! Without going into any further details, both of us would have been sacked for going anywhere near what was broadcast that day.

*****

Being an ex-player myself, I realise what some players can get up to, even today where much stricter rules are now par for the course. But that 'grip of the grape' can turn some into lunatics. Like the one about the Aussie who was staying at a nice hotel and decided it would be a good idea to shave off the hair of the eight-year-old son of the hotel manager.

Or the time when waiting in line to board a plane in Wellington, New Zealand, one player decided it was time to drop his old fella out and show his pierced member! Eddie was sure it was solid gold. The players get paid far too much these days.

And the one about the top England player who decided a touring Aussie international had abused his wife so he calmly asked for his hotel room key at reception and went up and rearranged a few things – including the player!

I remember that night well because I was having a nice drink in the bar with the great footballer Gordon Strachan who had attended that day's international clash against the Kangaroos. After a few drinks Gordon excused himself and left the bar, where I shouted out – rather loudly to impress Eddie and the boys – "Goodnight Gary" and for a split second the place went quiet only to erupt into laughter. I hid in the corner the rest of the night.

*****

It's not often you see Eddie get into an argument but he lost the plot one day in Australia before the England v PNG World Cup clash in 2008 in Townsville, Australia. It was a game that was so controversial because England were odds-on favourites to win and yet they were struggling and were 16-12 down at half time. Then things should have got worse when the Australian referee brought what should have been the winning try for PNG back for a forward pass which the replay showed was anything but forward.

It was an enthralling match that nearly didn't go to air for our Sky viewers in the UK. With one minute to go before the game kicked off, Eddie had the wrong feed in his ears and made it clear to the sound man it needed fixing NOW! Within seconds a slanging match got into full swing and as the time was ticking away, neither was backing off.

I looked on in amazement, mouth open, and before I could say anything Neville was between them both and screaming that we had only 20 seconds before going live!

"You fix it. You talk!" Neville yelled to both of them in turn.

When the cross came from the London studio five seconds later, Eddie dropped into his calm, collected mode as though nothing had happened. But it was close.

A few relaxing beers afterwards and we were all good mates again. TV is tense at times.

Another tense moment came in Neville's home town of Manly where we had the pleasure of staying in the Pacific Hotel right on the Manly Beach promenade which is a mixture of a holiday place and the warmth of a country village.

Almost next door is the famous Steyne Hotel, a great place to be seen and heard and where league fans congregate to 'chew the fat' in the back bar or have a good feed in the front lounge. Either way you can watch the surfers enjoying the waves whilst munching on a good burger – and I mean super-good seeing they have beetroot and a fried egg on top of the beef patty!

With the sun shining and the surf pounding into the golden sand, it's hard to ignore those amazing waves. But for Chris Sanderman, our Unit and Production Manager on that tour, it proved to be rather costly.

Chris made it clear he had surfed in Cornwall and that these big waves held no fear. So he waltzed out of the hotel, walked into a surf shop and purchased a brand spanking new surfboard.

I'm not being unkind to Mr Sanderman if I suggest he's a touch on the 'portly' side but in fairness, he had the muscle and strength to carry his new possession with quite some style past all the bikini-clad ladies and launched himself into the sea.

What happened next? I'm not quite sure, only he disappeared into the surf about 30 metres out whilst trying to stand up on the new surfboard. We finally caught sight of him being battered by a mighty wave and being pushed towards the beach. We then realised he didn't have one but TWO surfboards! Unfortunately his weight had just broken the bloody thing in half!

I know you shouldn't laugh at things like that but it was funny, and got even funnier when he tried to convince the bloke in the surf shop it was faulty and demanded his money back. We often saw him in the hotel pool after that!

One broken surfboard, one broken ego and one empty wallet.

That same tour saw me accused of speeding whilst driving back from the coastal town of Gosford to our hotel in Newcastle. The fine found its way back to England and the Sky offices three months later and I refused to accept I would do that sort of thing, only to be shown a photo which clearly showed my bald head.

I now wear a wig whilst driving overseas on tour.

24

Eddie: The Panda

I have said many times over the past quarter of a century that I have been blessed, and so I have.

I have a wonderful wife and family – Carole, Mark, Lisa, Sharon and my grandchildren Eleanor, Owen, Stephen and Isabella – who have supported me through thick and thin. The good times and the bad. I will love all of them until my dying day. And professionally I am fortunate in that there are not many in the business of sport on television who can look back on a career of over 30 unbroken years in the one sport on the one channel.

When Sky Sports came into being in the late 80s, nobody truly knew what the future held. No one knew whether it would be a hit or a miss. The fact of the matter is that throughout those years the company has grown into the biggest sports TV company in the entire world. It has been a privilege to have been a part of it – in at the beginning right the way through to the present day.

There are so many people to thank. All the people I have worked with, of course, including some special ones I'll come to in a minute. To the bosses, including John Davis right at the beginning at Champion Television, who had the guts to take a punt on me, to David Hill a gregarious Australian who fronted up the first Sky Sports service. He was a fantastic boss who arrived with an affinity for rugby league from his days down under. Obviously in those early traumatic days he fought for the sport and for us.

I'll never forget the day when, after I had finished recording a programme called *This is the Sports Channel* showcasing the best that the old BSB sports channel had to offer during the week, I wandered back into the office. The producer of the show had instructed me to go casual in front of the cameras with open necked shirts and pullovers. I'd bought a dozen of them for the run of the programme. Hilly was obviously watching the recording on a feed to a television set in his office and by the look on his face he was clearly unimpressed.

As I walked past his office he shouted my name at the top of his voice. I stopped in my tracks as he came out of the door. "Eddie," he said, "I don't want my rugby league commentator looking like a f***ing panda!" Then he turned on his heel and shut the door. The pullovers were taken back to the shop the moment I got back up north!

Following David was Vic Wakeling, who began running the sports news channel on BSB – *The Sports Centre* it was called. Vic survived the cull of the takeover and, after Hilly left for North America and Fox TV, he took over the reins of Sky Sports and did the job magnificently. It was Vic who successively renewed the Premier League football deal every time it came up. We all knew that the Premier League was the key to Sky's success and Vic made sure it was going nowhere else.

He also renewed the Rugby League contract year-on-year. Vic has always said that the rugby league team as a group has delivered good value for money and of course he also acknowledges that the sport has delivered too in bundles. It was Vic who signed the first Super League deal, approving the video referee idea in the process. It was Vic who rubber stamped the idea of the Grand Final to finish a season off in style and it was Vic who gave me one of the greatest pieces of advice.

The Super League was in the embryo stage with much talking behind closed doors. All very confidential of course. We were out shooting the links for *Boots 'n' All* in London one Tuesday afternoon when the news started to filter through that something was afoot. A move to the summer was by now on the cards and the idea was out of the bag. We had just finished our final link for the programme and the cameras had been put away. We were enjoying a coffee in a local café when the first news hit.

Nev was out producing the show with us and I proffered the idea that we must re-shoot some of the items and discuss the breaking news. "Nev," I said. "Our credibility is at stake here." Quite rightly Nev didn't want to rock any boats so he decided to ring back to base for some guidance. He got straight through to Mr Wakeling's office. "Vic, Eddie thinks that we MUST talk about this breaking news about a possible Super League on the show this week. His credibility is at stake."

I nodded. Nev had got the message across nicely. "Okay," said Nev, down the phone. "I'll tell him."

Obviously the negotiations between Sky and the Rugby Football League were, by now, at a crucial and delicate stage. No one as low down the food-chain as me could have realised just how delicate things were. But, come on ... my credibility WAS at stake. Nev looked at me and smiled wickedly. "I'll give it you word for word," he said. "Vic says you should stick your credibility up your arse!" Point taken. The show went to air as recorded. Super League was never mentioned again for a while. My credibility? I suppose I'm still looking for it!

Then there is Nev who has been in my ear and by my side all of these past 30 years. I mentioned earlier how he had taken a big gamble in coming over from Australia in the first place as a freelance cameraman and backed his own talent to make an impact. He began working alongside John Davis as an assistant but he obviously had an eye for the main job. His was the camera plan that was adopted, and in the end his was the directing style that has made Sky's rugby league coverage so special and innovative.

You see Nev has been a league fan all his life. He still makes every effort to watch his beloved Manly in the NRL every week. He has a breadth of knowledge second only to Ian Proctor who has been another very special member of our team. Ian is the best statistician and history man in the game.

Ian researches every match we do. He can tell you anything and everything about anyone in the game you might care to name. His knowledge is unbelievable and he's been at my side just about every game we have done. He nudges me on the arm, I pull back the headphones, Ian whispers a piece of classic info into my shell-like and in an instant out of my mouth it comes. He's come to be known as 'Eddie's Brain'. He's that and more and has made my life so easy in that commentary box.

But back to Nev. Here's a bloke who really has made an impact on his chosen sport. The video referee and the Grand Final itself are just two nuggets among a host of innovation. The way the game is covered is superb, his pictures zing along. Whether it's Wigan-Saints, the Hull derby or a more mundane fixture between teams struggling at the bottom end of the table, it doesn't matter. He has the knack of being able to tell a brilliant televisual story. He is now the Head of Rugby League at Sky – so well deserved for a guy who was told once that a Saturday night Old Trafford Grand Final under floodlights at teatime could quite possibly kill the game! How right you were Nev – much of our success is down to you old thing!

And then of course there's the lad himself, Stevo, our very own bald eagle who has been there through thick and thin all of these years. How very different things would have been without him. It wouldn't have been the same, that's for sure and certainly not as good.

In many ways Stevo is an enigma. He has taken most of the flak from the players, coaches, fans and viewers. I've lost count now of the number of phone calls I've had from coaches complaining about something he's said. Of course, because I'm alongside him I very often get daubed with the same brush. A lot of the stuff he says I get the blame for and some of the stuff I say – thanks to Ian – he takes the credit for!

People should remember Stevo has first of all given up 25 years of his family life to working for Sky Sports and rugby league. Oh I know food has to be put on the table and all that, but he has spent the best part of the last quarter of a century on the other side of the world from his wife and daughters. That in itself is big ask. I often joke that I've seen more of him than his missus and I suppose I have – nine months of the year over here and less than three months back home. I really believe that I should never have married him in the first place!

But it has been a partnership made in rugby league heaven. We would never have made some of those crazy moments, never had some of the quips and malapropisms that are now the stuff of legend and most importantly we would never have had so much fun.

He played the game at the very highest level. He won a League title as skipper with little Dewsbury, when they beat Leeds in the 1972-73 Championship Final, and picked up the Harry Sunderland trophy in the process. He was a World Cup winner of course in France in 1972, scoring a try in the final against Australia. He then played in Australia for Penrith Panthers after a then world record transfer fee of £20,000 was paid for his services. When he finished playing he worked in the Australian media before coming over to join the satellite revolution and of course the rest is history.

He also established a museum of the history of the game twice. The first time was in Australia, which was hugely successful, and the second was over here in the UK. He has done so much for the benefit of the game. What isn't so widely known is all the charity work he does quietly behind the scenes. He has helped countless charities throughout the land with his time and effort raising hundreds of thousands of pounds.

He's in the Roll of Honour at Rugby League HQ but so am I now, having 'retired' as the host of the Man of Steel Awards night. In 2015 the game did me the great honour of enrolling me, the highest accolade for a non-player in the game, I am told. How proud am I? But I've done a quarter of the good that he has done. Sir Stevo? I think so, but then again his knees probably wouldn't let him get down on the floor for the sword to be placed on his shoulders, so we can rule that one out!

What I can say is that Stevo, even though he finished playing over 40 years ago, is still the most recognisable figure within the game throughout the length and breadth of the UK – and Europe too. People are always coming up to him and saying: "Hey aren't you that bald bloke off the telly who does the rugby?" And of course he is. What's more, no matter what they say to him he always gives them time and they remember him for that of course.

For the record I'm the one who's been alongside him all these years and NO, I DON'T DYE MY HAIR! Let me get that straight once and for all.

Let me also say thanks to the great game of rugby league, to Sky, the players, the coaches, the administrators of the game and all the fans.

But most of all thanks to my old mate Stevo. It has been a blast!

25

Stevo: It's Been Grand

It's been an amazing journey alongside one of the nicest blokes you will ever meet. OK, I call him a snob and he agrees wholeheartedly. In fact he often suggests he should have rampant lions on either side of his driveway and fountains at the bottom of the garden.

He does have an outside hot tub in his large garden and one day a couple of horses actually wandered in and took quite a while to eject.

It's been a lot of fun working with Eddie and, apart from a couple of tiffs, we have got on well together and both our families have the greatest respect for each other.

He has wonderful children and I remember the first time I met his son Mark, a loveable young lad with a keen and eager brain who, at a tender age, never stopped asking questions and was mature beyond his 12 years. As he grew older he turned his hand to music, singing and the theatre and not surprisingly became bloody good at them all. Eddie and Carole could never understand why he often screamed out loud when he was anywhere near me but I have to confess, any chance I had I would dig him in the ribs, and not too lightly either.

I still call him 'Ribs' to this day which confuses his girlfriend no end. In fact when he had his 21st birthday I bought him a watch engraved 'to Ribs' which he still wears with pride. He's a thoroughly nice lad, a credit to his family and a bundle of fun, always with a smile on his face.

*****

Over the years, Eddie has laughed more than a few times at some of my remarks on air. Even to this day he has no idea what I will say next … come to think of it neither do I! We once did a commentary at Warrington where we called the two props the wrong way round for the entire game. It wasn't until we climbed down the steep ladder that we found out. An old bloke was waiting there to inform us we had mucked up.

Another Warrington game saw the home side take ages to come out after half time. The camera was pointing down the empty tunnel so Neville the director opted to get away from a 'dead' shot and focused on the cheerleaders going through an acrobatic routine. The trouble was Eddie was standing and couldn't see what was on screen as the cameraman zoomed into one of the girls doing a cartwheel which didn't leave much to the imagination.

At that same moment Eddie said: "Fancy a bash at that Stevo?"

I replied tongue-in-cheek: "You mean the cartwheel don't you?"

I don't think I've heard Neville's voice as loud as he screamed in my ear: "Another word from you and you'll never work in television again!"

On one occasion it was a cold night at Headingly and both of us were shivering on the gantry when I tried my best to call out Ellery Hanley who was playing for Leeds when I was amazed to see my top set of teeth fly out, hit the desk and drop on to the floor. I quickly dived down into the gloom to search for them whilst Eddie cracked up and couldn't speak. Now two minutes is a long time in TV and all I could hear was Nev yet again screaming: "Will one of you at least start to talk!"

We couldn't, it was so funny yet embarrassing for yours truly, but the gnasher's didn't break so the commentary finally got underway again.

Leeds has been a nightmare at times because of the spiral staircase that was built, would you believe, in front of the South Stand where the most ardent fans stand up for the game. To walk up it was a nightmare as not only was abuse thrown at you, so were coins (of low value – remember they are Yorkshire folk), sweets, pebbles and whatever they could lay their hands on. More than a few missiles made their mark but one day a young kid topped the lot. He was standing at the bottom of the spiral steps and asked me for my autograph when before I knew it he showered me with a handful of Midget Gems, those hard, tiny chewable fruit-flavoured sweets, and one hit me in the eye. Eddie and I only had three minutes whilst the advertisements were playing to get to the studio which was situated in the corner of the stadium about 60 yards away.

Never mind the bloody studio I wasn't going to be treated in that way, so I took after this kid, caught him and gave him a piece of my mind while all the while he was shouting he'd tell his dad. I yelled out: "I'll word your dad too you little sod!" I just made the studio in time and dad never turned up.

But the worst happened on a lovely spring day where, as I was entering the studio, a house brick bounced off the door as I was closing it. Bloody hell, I thought, that was aimed at me, and felt somewhat uneasy at doing the half time talk. When I came out of the studio the police were wrestling with a bloke on the floor and one of them asked if I wanted to press charges.

"No, just throw the lunatic out of the ground."

To my amazement they said they'd turfed him out half an hour earlier because he was walking about with a brick in his hand and had paid again to have another go at me! Eddie of course was laughing his head off.

I got my own back at St Helens where at the old Knowsley Road ground the trek to the studio was through the loyal Saints fans. The walkway to the studio was on a lower level which enabled those fans leaning against the crush barriers to have a fine old time slapping my bald head as we rushed towards what was a garden shed! I'm sure the fans had a laugh about it but by the time I got there my bloody head was red raw.

"What's up with you?" said Eddie. "They don't mean any harm."

This had gone on for a few years and I dreaded having to run the gauntlet of 'no harm' until one day guess what they focused on? The long-nosed one!

As soon as Eddie hit the studio he was screaming over his microphone: "Nev we need security we have been attacked!" Attack? No, just that his dyed hair had been ruffled.

At the next home game at Saints, two burly policemen were waiting to escort us and you can imagine the reaction from the crowd, all hell was let loose. It now became even more of a challenge for the fans to try and get to us both whilst evading being snared by the coppers! One PC stood outside the studio to ensure no fans could get near us and then the other escorted us back to the stairs, up to the gantry. Saints hadn't played all that well in the first half and I didn't realise he had been listening to how I was slagging them off at half time, so when I came out of the studio he chipped me and said: "You can make your own way back!"

Fans can get a little bit out of hand from time to time and

I've received the odd death threat in the post. One bloke from Widnes threatened if he ever saw me in the town, he'd drive on to the pavement then run over me and reverse enough times to ensure I was dead!

You should ignore such people but on this occasion I replied because he had actually put his address and postcode on the letter. I replied saying I was a sporting chappie and could he send me details of his car make and colour. A week later I received in the post a photo of him leaning against the car with the words: "This is me and the car that's going to kill you." You can't beat them all.

David Howes was another bloke who got me into some bother. David had worked at the RFL for many years and we became good friends. So good that when he took up the position of CEO at St Helens, he thought it a good idea to get one of the ex-players who entertained the crowd to wind up the fans by shouting: "Come on everybody, let's give Stevo a nice welcome". You can imagine the noise of the booing from all corners of the stadium. But I have broad shoulders and handled it, despite it making things uncomfortable.

But Howsie overstepped the mark one day just a week before we covered a game when he posted cowboy-style posters about the town featuring my photo and the words: "REWARD-ALIVE OR DEAD ... STEVO". It cost him one hell of an expensive lunch but we are still good mates.

Many years earlier that same club actually sent a letter to Vic Wakeling who was then Head of Sport stating that although Sky would be welcome to broadcast games, Mike Stephenson was banned and not allowed into the ground. A quick phone call to the club from Vic saying that's OK but they wouldn't be getting any more Sky money soon had them backtracking and suggesting someone had got hold of the official letterheaded paper without their knowledge.

Wakefield's Belle Vue ground was another that nearly

finished us all off. We were getting ready ten minutes before going on air when there was a creaking sound and within seconds the entire gantry collapsed ... and dropped thankfully only a couple of feet! We were all shaken and it took a while for us to get composed again. Dave Redfern, the floor manager, shouted out the best escape was out through the window ... a drop of 30 feet. No way! I tested the now broken floor to see if what was left could handle my weight – which thankfully it did – and we all escaped to eventually start the show from the side-lines. It still resulted in the lights and cameras being wrecked. Thankfully the only injury was a sprained wrist suffered by one of the cameramen!

So it hasn't always been easy in our world of television.

I know I'm forthright in my opinions and I know some people get upset but I just call it as I see it. A spade is a spade, although a lot of coaches, players and officials collar poor Eddie who often gets blamed for what I have said. But whatever you think I don't make it up. To his credit, Eddie gives them my personal mobile number but not many ring me.

Sometimes I get stopped by a player and told I got it wrong – a knock-on, forward pass, whatever – I just ask them to watch the replay and get back to me but no one ever does.

Having played for a long time both here in the UK and in Australia, I know what it's like to get on the wrong side of the media, especially in Sydney. Boy they like to have a go at you when you are a pommy playing down under – and yes, of course I have had bad games and had to accept the truth. Sadly a few players won't accept criticism.

Most players do take it on the chin though. One particular international was hacked off at some of the things I said when he had a poor game and wanted a right of reply.

When we met up I gave him a sheet of paper and asked him to write down on the right side all the bad things he thought I had said about him. He got to about four or five and handed the sheet back. I then started to write all the good things about him that I had said over the years and I was about to turn the paper over before he shook my hand and said point taken.

*****

Despite the occasional 'difficult' games we've had to cover, Eddie and I have had some wonderful times. When we started to call the Wembley Finals we were so excited and enjoyed each one, especially on the Friday in London before the game. At that time Silk Cut had become the major sponsors of the Challenge Cup Final and they pushed the boat out big time with a function where money was no object and to be invited was the dream ticket.

All the rugby league media would attend and the major buzz was trying to work out where the function was being held. It was always a secret so we had to wait in our hotels until the coaches arrived to whisk us away to a night of good food and wine.

The first one I attended was at the Natural History Museum where we were seated in among the dinosaurs. It was a brilliant evening and later in the night each table had to take their turn to go up on a stage and sing a song.

The first year I was on a table with the great journalist, my old mate John Robinson and his lovely wife Maureen. We had a superb time but I don't think we were in the running for best song. However, it was the start of many years of 'where are we going next year?'

A few years later was the first time I saw Eddie drunk. After the function we decided to have a tipple in the hotel bar to top the night off and I suspect someone spiked Eddie's drink. It took four of us to carry him to his room. I'd never seen him in that state before and not since.

One year the do was at Madame Tussauds, which was hilarious because most of the ladies thought it good fun to have their photos taken with Linford Christie. His wax effigy was, shall we say, well-endowed and that particular part of his anatomy was well polished by midnight!

It was so much fun and each year Silk Cut tried to outdo the previous year's effort which was becoming difficult. Probably the best was at the Savoy Hotel, and boy did they push the boat out on that one. For entertainment they had a Shirley Bassey impersonator who was so good one of the older Journos wouldn't be convinced she wasn't the real thing, and bold as brass approached her for a photo and an autograph. Bless her she signed it: "Best Wishes, Shirley Bassey".

I enjoyed it so much I went to the toilet after the show, fell asleep and got woken up by the cleaners at 6.00 the following morning.

Another hotel moment was when a former international player came out of the lift the Sunday morning after the Wembley Final to check out, only for his suitcase to burst open and reveal ten hotel engraved coat hangers spilling towards the main desk. He of course declined to pay and handed them back to the receptionist, stating someone had put them in without his knowledge. Very funny and ten out of ten for lying.

I often talk about Yorkshiremen being careful with their money but at that same hotel it wasn't just me who was put out by the price of the beer and wine in the hotel bar. The prices were outrageous but not for another international who had brought in two six-packs and hid them under his lounge chair. He then coughed loudly every time he opened a can to cover up the hiss! They were lively functions that had some of the quietest people becoming totally outrageous.

Unfortunately at one of the Wembley Fridays I found out that my mother had been diagnosed with terminal cancer. It shook me to the bone and I went on a bender by drinking at lunchtime and through the afternoon so that I was in a right state by the time the function started.

When I walked into the function hall I walked across to Eddie's table, kissed him and we both fell to the floor. Worse was to come when the entertainment started. It was a live orchestra where they invited people up to play certain instruments of which I decided the big timpani drum was ideal for a man in my state.

A few tried to steer me away, including Eddie, but I was on the stage as quick as a flash. The conductor came over and showed me what to do when he pointed the baton at me which I did, and after three mighty blows the bloody drum split and I fell into it!

As for what happened after that I have no idea, but amazingly I woke up on Saturday no worse for wear and with no hangover.

Back in those days we couldn't show the Wembley Final live, although we called it as live and it went out at about 10.30 that same night. After a few years doing this, Nev decided we should let some of the younger breed have a go at calling the Final and Ben Proe got his chance. Ben did a good job of it, allowing Eddie and me to just press the flesh at the pre-match lunch and enjoy the game and we have done that ever since.

One such lunch was in the Wembley Great Hall where Eddie and I sat with Nev and Vic. We found ourselves positioned quite close to the top table where the honoured guest was Elisabeth Murdoch who at that time was the Managing Director of BSkyB.

Just after the main course I felt a strong hand on my right shoulder where what looked like a bouncer whispered in my ear: "Elisabeth Murdoch would like a word with you after lunch."

I laughed and thought Eddie had put this bloke up to it and politely told him to sod off, only for the look on Eddie, Nev and Vic's faces to convince me it was serious. They froze and so did I but their eyes were telling me 'behave yourself'. So off I went to the top table and had a good five minutes talking to the head of the company who was so friendly and introduced me to her new husband. She said I was doing a great job and informed me that her father was an avid follower of rugby league and passed on his best wishes!

Wow, I couldn't believe it! And neither could the others when I was greeted back to the table by three blokes whispering: "What did she say?" Or more to the point: "What the hell did you say?"

Jokingly I said she wanted to double my contract which sent Vic white, but I couldn't hold a straight face and laughed out loud and the colour came back to Vic's cheeks.

It was a very nice gesture and it's something I will never forget.

The day after I read that Rupert Murdoch's wedding present to the newly wed couple was a radio station in the USA. Nice work if you can get it.

Like I have said, these functions at Wembley and the Silk Cut Friday nights were becoming legendary and when we arrived at the following year's Friday night bonanza we found out that the venue was Chelsea Barracks. All the waiters were dressed as cowboys and they gave us cap guns to fire at each other during the dinner. The entire joint was dressed up like the *Gunfight at the OK Corral*, It was great fun and noisy but not for the Boss of the RFL, Maurice

Lyndsey, who for some unknown reason allowed himself to be strapped to a spinning wheel where a bloke in an Apache outfit came out and produced a bundle of sharp knives.

Everyone held their breath as this bloke threw all of them with great precision and skill at the RFL boss who, I can assure you, wasn't best pleased despite his fixed grin. Not one knife hit where most of the crowd wanted them to. You can imagine the comments the crowd were crying out!

Many people disliked Maurice because of his association with the mighty Wigan, who had been the first club to go full-time professional way before Super League started – and not surprisingly they won all before them.

When he virtually forced the clubs to accept Rupert Murdoch's money, I admired him for his guts and stance over the issue, because to me he saved our game from going backwards. He was strong when he had to be but he could be a pleasure to be with and Eddie and I have many happy memories of being in his company. One such occasion was when we were in Australia and he invited quite a few of the journos and a few retired international stars back to his suite at the hotel. We not only enjoyed his hospitality with plenty to drink but, unbeknown to Maurice, some were ringing England on his room phone. God knows how much his bill would have been but I knew one ex player who was on there for well over half an hour!

Maurice knew how to get publicity and realised TV was a great way to project our game. Every time we requested his presence for a news interview or to be on our *Boots 'n' All* show, he never refused. And when the newspapers in London failed to give rugby league any publicity, he would board a train to the big smoke and meet up with the sports editors of the national press and ask simply: 'Why?'

Obviously our game has had a few problems but when needed Maurice would never shy away from letting the general public know that any issues would be sorted out quickly. Not all bosses at the RFL have had that sort of outlook but I think it's better to front up for the camera when the fans want answers.

I have had a number of run-ins with people at the RFL. I realise it's a hard job to run such an organisation but I never hit it off with Richard Lewis. He did a great job in fixing up the financial side of the game, but he always seemed reluctant to talk to the press and TV. I felt he could have done so much more to promote the game.

The current Chief Executive Nigel Wood has his detractors but I find him honest and I like him because he's a straightforward bloke. I think it helps that he did play rugby league and knows the value of public relations and keeping the fans on board. He makes himself available to the media, although some of his suggestions are from left-field. One was giving a bonus point to a team winning at half time, which prompted me to say live on air that whoever thought of that was a lunatic! Apparently Nigel's mother was none too pleased. I'm sure there are also plenty of people at the RFL who disagree with my opinions and no doubt they won't be inviting me to their corporate barbecue any time soon!

*****

So who would I invite to 'my' barbecue? Eddie and Nev of course and our good friend Ian Proctor would get a gold-edged invite card for sure. And also many others at Sky including the cameramen, riggers, technicians who have been together for years and have helped me along the way. I thank them all from the bottom of my heart which will piss them off as I'm sure they would rather I buy them a drink. One day I will, I promise.

Sue Goldstone, the make-up lady who has endured nightmares trying to make me look good on TV for over 20 years and who is such a nice person she would also be on the list. As would David Redfern who was a teammate in the 1972 successful World Cup side and has been a floor manager for many years.

David took over the role from the admirable Peter Judge – another on my guest list – who stumbled, fumbled but made it all work in any studio we worked in. I met Peter many years ago when he worked for Silk Cut on those extravagant functions and was so pleased when he came to work at Sky. Unlike many others, Peter and I only fell out once and it happened when England played France in a one-off Test. I decided to head over to France early and take a couple of days off in the south west, an area famous for prunes and wine. The former I can give a miss but the latter is another story. I soon became friendly with the bar on the corner across from my hotel and spent three nights on the trot trying to make myself understood in French and failing badly. But the atmosphere was amazing and the owner and his wife made me very welcome, as did the regulars.

As it turned out it became a blessing that I had become friendly with them for they saved the day – or should I say the night – after the game had finished at the stadium. We were booked into the dining room at the stadium for dinner only to find the brass band had told them they were from Sky and scoffed what should have been our meal.

In desperation I raced back to the corner bar and, despite it being nearly midnight, I asked if they could do meals for 20 people. To my surprise and relief the patron rang upstairs to his wife who was in bed and she came down and cooked steak and frites for us all.

Whilst the smell of cooking permeated from the kitchen

I showed our make-up lady Sue how to play the pinball machine and in doing so had my arms either side of her showing how the flippers worked. Peter took umbrage at this and stormed off, giving both Sue and me a right mouthful. "Make that 19 meals please," I shouted. Peter didn't talk to me for a few days but we had a laugh about it eventually and moved on.

There have been a number of great cameramen who have worked with us over the years. I can't mention them all here but two stick out like Eddie's nose. One is a close friend of Neville's from Australia, Mark McAfferty, and the other is Andrew McDonald. Both are among the best in the business and they've worked on countless top world sporting events including the summer and winter Olympics. They also have my respect through their ability to drink me under the table! I'm sure they both have hollow legs, and such is their camaraderie that there have been a few times we've gone for a nightcap only to exit the bar with the sun rising the following morning. They're both great fun but they can make a severe mess of your wallet as well as your liver!

Kevin Connor, our production manager at Sky Sports, will always be welcome because he's a fount of knowledge and does a great job ensuring our outside broadcasts do what they're supposed to do ... broadcast.

Another who would be welcome to chuck a few prawns on the grill is Assistant Producer Mark Smith. Mark was barely out of his teens when I took him to Tenerife for a week's holiday and whilst in mid-air he made it quite clear he wasn't going on a drinking marathon. Funnily enough he finished up drunk as a skunk before lunch on the first day. Never think a big glass of orange juice for breakfast is without Vodka. He asked me twice if his drink was off as it tasted funny. By noon he was off and very funny!

We took to drinking in a great bar near the hotel run by a

gay guy, Pasquell, who had a liking for Mark's good looks and blond hair. He was a friendly guy so we invited him to join us on his day off while we lounged around the hotel pool enjoying the odd beer. At one point, Mark stood up saying he was going for a swim. We watched as he stood on the pool side flexing his muscles before diving in, only for Pasquell to say he wanted to swim too. In mid-air Mark had heard this and proceeded to break Mark Spitz's record for the 100 metres then quickly exited the pool at the other end before poor Pasquell could rearrange his swimwear.

It's one of the funniest things I have ever seen in my life.

And last of all my appreciation to a number of people who deserve recognition. Eddie has explained in more detail about our medical problems and I'd certainly like to thank all those doctors, nurses and medical staff who have helped us both get back to health. Not least, Dr. Schilling who fixed my heart problem and for that I'm truly grateful.

Thanks also to Professor Timothy Briggs, one of Europe's finest from the National Orthopaedic Hospital in Stanmore, who fitted me with a new hip just recently. Professor Briggs assures me by the time you read this book I will be disco dancing once again!

To all those physios, trainers, massage men and women, kit men and hangers on for helping me through some rough times back in my playing days.

And of course, to all my family: Maureen, Craig, Hayley, Kayley, Alyssa and my grandchildren Holly, Archie and Harry. Also to my friends too numerous to mention and not forgetting fans that have liked me – and even those who have hated me. Every one of you has been part of a great adventure. I like to think I will retire with the knowledge I have tried my best, been honest and done a decent job, but it wouldn't have been possible without all your support, so thanks to you all. It's been grand.

Afterword

When I got asked to write the Afterword (is there such a thing?) for Eddie and Stevo's book, I originally thought of all sorts of 'funny' things to write: "Congratulations on making it this far. Did you get the hardback because it will wear harder holding up your fridge?" You know the sort of thing.

I've decided instead that to do so would be a disservice to two men who I have the utmost respect for, and to whom in many ways I have been as close as many members of my own family.

Eddie, Stevo and myself, along with Ian Proctor, have shared over a quarter of a century of the best working environment and atmosphere anyone could wish for. We have been at the heart of a 'family'. Like all families we squabble, huff with each other, have little (or major) tantrums and generally fall out regularly. We also laugh, play together and love each other like any true family. My constant mantra throughout my time running the rugby league department has been that I get paid to go to the footy with my mates.

At the very heart of that are Eddie and Stevo. Be under no illusions, theirs has always been the hardest job on the team. They, along with most television presenters, get ridiculed and revered in pretty equal measure. They get blamed for every mistake we make. It is their job to be the front window of our presentation and commentary, with their every word measured and dissected by the fans, the public and their colleagues in the written media.

I always say if you think you can do a better job, give it a go. Grab a mate, sit in front of a match and record yourself to the coverage. Call every player accurately, predict every play, incisively analyse each and every move, be entertaining and informative at all times and ensure a great viewing experience for the fans glued to their television. Can you do it?

Do Eddie and Stevo do all of that all the time? Of course not, they're human, but I guarantee you that over nearly 30 years together they have delivered each and every one of those facets in abundance, and on those occasions – a Grand Final, an outstanding victory for Great Britain or simply the Wide to West moment – when all the stars are aligned, and all these skills and talents come together, Eddie and Stevo are a juggernaut of sporting entertainment unmatched in the annals of television commentary.

Am I biased? Of course I am. We're talking about two of my best friends here. Two people I have journeyed with through what has become a lifetime on a mission. The two things that unite Eddie, Stevo, Ian and myself are a pure desire for the sport we love to survive and thrive. At the same time they never take themselves too seriously and are always conscious that they are part of a bigger team.

There has never been any question of the 'star' element that can plague a production, and they are always aware and appreciative of the massive infrastructure that starts with the cable being laid and finishes with the PA counting us off air. And they know and have a chat and a laugh with every member of the 80-odd crew that it takes to put a Super League match on air.

I hope you've enjoyed the book and their stories. Some of them may even have a factual grounding. One thing I know, with the retirement of Stevo and therefore the brand of Eddie 'n' Stevo, Sky Sports and rugby league will never be the same again.

They truly have earned their place in rugby league history. Good luck guys, it's been a blast!

Neville Smith, Head of Rugby League, Sky Sports